MASTERING CAREER SKILLS

Organization Skills

Mastering Career Skills

Communication Skills

Organization Skills

Professional Ethics and Etiquette

Research and Information Management

FERGUSON

MASTERING CAREER SKILLS

Organization
Skills

☑Checkmark Books®
An imprint of Infobase Publishing

Mastering Career Skills: Organization Skills

Copyright © 1998, 2004 by Infobase Publishing

Checkmark Books
An imprint of Infobase Publishing
132 West 31st Street
New York NY 10001

ISBN-10: 0-8160-7116-0
ISBN-13: 978-0-8160-7116-6

Organization skills.—2nd ed.
  p. cm.—(Career skills library)
Rev. ed. of: Organization skills / by Richard Worth. c1998.
Includes bibliographical references and index.
Contents: Principles of time-management—Managing your schedule—
Eliminating time wasters—The pitfalls of procrastination—Organizing your
workplace—Seven secrets of better time management.
  ISBN 0-8160-5521-1 (hc)—ISBN 0-8160-7116-0 (pb)
  1. Time management. 2. Scheduling. [1. Time management. 2. Vocational
guidance.] I. Worth, Richard. Organization skills. II. J.G. Ferguson
Publishing Company. III. Series.
  HD69.T54W68 2004
  650.1—dc22   2003015062

Checkmark Books are available at special discounts when purchased in bulk quantities for businesses, associations, institutions, or sales promotions. Please call our Special Sales Department in New York at (212) 967-8800 or (800) 322-8755.

You can find Facts On File on the World Wide Web at
http://www.factsonfile.com

Text design by David Strelecky
Cover design by Salvatore Luongo

Printed in the United States of America

MP FOF 10 9 8 7 6 5 4 3 2 1

This book is printed on acid-free paper.

CONTENTS

Introduction 1

1 Principles of Time Management 7

2 Managing Your Schedule 25

3 Eliminating Time Wasters 47

4 The Pitfalls of Procrastination 67

5 Organizing Your Workplace 87

6 Seven Secrets of Better Time
   Management. 108

Glossary 128

Bibliography 132

Index 135

INTRODUCTION

All of us belong to organizations. Perhaps you are a member of a club or athletic team or have a part-time job in an organization such as a fast-food restaurant or a clothing store. Your parents probably work for organizations, too. These organizations may be large companies, such as a manufacturing plant, or much smaller firms, such as a travel agency. Some organizations run very smoothly. They are tidy and efficient, and everything is usually done promptly. Others are just the opposite—they are untidy and disorganized. Within them, nothing ever seems to be accomplished on time. The difference in the workings of efficient and inefficient organizations lies in the use of organizational skills across the group, no matter how big or small.

Individuals are the same way. Some of them always seem to be running late and never finish anything on schedule. Others are well organized. What is the main difference between organized and unorganized people? Their use of time. Organized people do not waste time. However, this doesn't mean that they have to be working constantly. Organized people give themselves plenty of time for recreation or quiet reflection. But they also seem to get more tasks done—more short-term assignments and long-term projects.

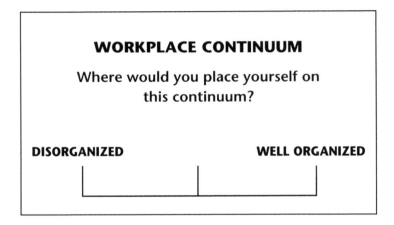

WORKPLACE CONTINUUM

Where would you place yourself on this continuum?

DISORGANIZED   **WELL ORGANIZED**

There is an old saying: "If you want something done, give it to a busy person." Well-organized people know how to fit a variety of projects into their schedules. They know how to get them done and how to do them successfully.

Today, employers are looking for people who can handle a number of responsibilities. Like accomplished jugglers, workers must be able to keep several balls in the air at the same time and prevent them from falling. This takes organization skills. You can't wait to learn these skills on the job. Employers expect you to arrive there with them.

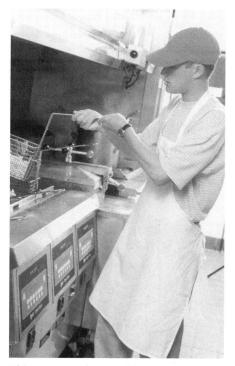

FACT

Since 1990, more than 30 percent of all workers have been laid off largely due to downsizings. Those who remain are expected to do more than ever before.

This young worker uses his organization skills to balance a part-time fast-food job and a full college courseload. (Corbis)

How do you develop organization skills? Many people begin learning them in school. They practice organizing important day-to-day tasks that need to be accomplished on time. These include homework assignments, extracurricular activities, and part-time jobs. Organization skills are relatively easy to master.

Today, employers are looking for people who can handle a number of responsibilities.

Perfecting them does not take hours of practice, like playing the piano or perfecting a golf swing does. However, you must get into the habit of establishing regular routines for yourself and sticking to them.

Most important, you will find the rewards of being organized to be almost immediate: more control of your life, a greater sense of accomplishment, and a higher level of success. These are just some of the benefits of organizing your time and using it to the utmost.

Good order is the foundation of all good things.

—Edmund Burke, British political theorist

This book will help you realize the benefits of good organizational skills. The advice here will help you become more organized so that you will get the most out of your school, work, and personal time. The following are some of the topics covered in this book:

- Building time-management skills that will teach you to prioritize, be on time, and have more time

- Creating an effective to-do list and a weekly schedule that incorporates goals you have set for yourself

- Avoiding everyday "time wasters" such as unnecessary telephone calls and Internet use

TIME-MANAGEMENT QUESTIONS

Do you generally get up in the morning on time?

Do you usually have time for breakfast?

Do you catch the school bus in the morning?

Are you late for your first class?

Do you finish your homework assignments promptly?

Do you use study halls to complete tomorrow's work?

Are you on time for extracurricular activities?

Can you find papers in your desk or room at home?

Are you usually late or on time for your part-time job?

Do you complete job assignments promptly?

■ Changing your habits and stopping yourself from getting bogged down by procrastination

■ Avoiding mess and clutter in your workspace through the use of a filing system and other organization techniques

■ Enhancing your time-management skills so that all areas of your life become more organized

1

PRINCIPLES OF TIME MANAGEMENT

"**A**nd that concludes our training program," the instructor said, picking up her notes. "Oh, one more thing. Don't forget that each of you is making a presentation to top management Thursday morning. It's your chance to shine and show them what you have learned, so be prepared!"

Bill rose and started to leave. "I'm glad that's over," he whispered to Evan. They had sat together during the entire program.

"Yeah, but there's still that presentation," Evan told him. "Mine's almost done. How are you doing?"

"Oh, I'll get around to it," Bill answered confidently. "But not today."

Bill returned to his office and found a pile of telephone messages and faxes on his chair. He also read several important emails from clients that required immediate action on his part. It was almost 6:00 P.M. by the time he'd answered all the requests. As Bill looked at the clock, he realized that he was supposed to have a report on his boss's desk by the end of the day. He had had a week to do it. That had seemed like so much time. Bill figured he could put it off. What a mistake!

He rushed around his office, trying to gather all the figures for the report. Everything he needed wasn't there, but he couldn't help that now. Maybe his boss wouldn't notice. Bill typed away furiously for several hours. By the time he'd finished, it was almost midnight. He walked briskly into his boss's office and left the report on his desk. "Better late than never," Bill told himself.

The next day he was exhausted. But he had telephone calls to make all morning, faxes and emails to reply to, a long sales meeting to attend, and a full afternoon of catching up on paperwork. It was almost 6:30 by the time Bill had finished. He was heading home when his boss caught him at the elevator.

"Look," his boss said, shaking his head, "this report you gave me is incomplete. You'll have to stay here tonight and rewrite it. I need it on my desk first thing in the morning."

Bill wanted to ask for a little more time, but he knew the report was already late and his boss was in no mood to listen to any excuses. Reluctantly, he walked toward his office, passing Evan in the hallway.

"See you tomorrow, Bill," Evan said. "Remember, 8:00 sharp. We have to give our presentations."

Bill had completely forgotten about the presentations. Now he had a report to finish and a talk to prepare for top management. He slumped in his chair and started to work. Five hours later, Bill had finished the report, but he was completely worn out. "I'll just put my head on the desk for a few moments," he thought, figuring that a little rest was all he needed to tackle his presentation. The next time he looked at the clock it was 7:00 A.M.

NOT ENOUGH TIME

Today, most people in the workplace have a lot to do but not enough time in which to do it. Many workers talk about always running behind, or they complain that there are not enough hours in the day. Corporate downsizings have placed more pressure on everyone. As thousands of workers are laid off, those who remain are asked to take on greater responsibilities. One woman in the public relations department of a large manufacturing company has seen the staff cut by more than half. She's working longer hours and still has trouble getting everything done.

The solution to many of these headaches is good use of time-management skills. If you procrastinate and don't organize your time well, you'll end up the way Bill did.

Not only do today's employees have more to do; the nature of work has changed.

FACT

According to a recent Families and Work Institute survey, both men and women wish they worked about 11 fewer hours per week.

Not only do today's employees have more to do; the nature of work has changed. "Jobs aren't structured the way they used to be," explains human resources director Lisa Law. "Every job has more components to it. You can't specialize and you need to manage your time."

Law points out that in her company, an accounts receivable clerk used to receive a bill, code it, and pass it on to someone else to check its accuracy. Now a clerk is expected to put the information from the bill on a computer and check it himself. If the charges are incorrect, he must find out the reason and correct it. What's more, all of this work must be completed within a tight deadline. "These things take time-management and organization skills," Law says.

Because jobs are more complex than ever, workers must master more information to do them.

Because jobs are more complex than ever, workers must master more information to do them. Never before has so much information been available from so many sources. Books, magazines, television, and the Internet provide us with enormous amounts of data. We need an opportunity to access it, evaluate it, and figure out what to use. This puts even more pressure on us to use time effectively.

Yet, we live in an age where there never seems to be enough time. Technologies such as fax machines and email enable us to communicate instantaneously. And the expectation is that we should do everything rapidly, packing as much as possible into each day.

According to a recent report in the *New York Times,* adolescents may be trying to do so much that they

HOW WELL ARE YOU SLEEPING?

According to a report in the *New York Times,* the average person needs 8.3 hours of sleep per night. Most people get between 7.0 and 7.5 hours, and nearly 40 million Americans suffer from chronic sleep disorders and wakefulness.

The National Sleep Foundation also reports that Americans are getting too little sleep, making them irritable and impatient. According to the poll results, about 47 million Americans don't get enough sleep to stay alert in the daytime. Approximately 58 percent of respondents reported either difficulty falling asleep, waking a lot during the night, waking up too early and not being able to get back to sleep, or feeling unrefreshed at least a few nights a week. People who are sleepy are found to be more likely to make mistakes.

are not getting enough sleep. Difficult class schedules, extracurricular activities, part-time jobs, and volunteer work are leaving students groggy and affecting their grades. As Jan Farrington writes in *Career World* magazine, there is never enough time to do everything. "You will always have to make choices about how you spend the time you have."

ORGANIZING YOUR TIME AND YOUR WORK

"If I only had a little more time." This statement is often heard from people who don't know how to use their time efficiently. How we organize our time often determines how successful we will be, not how much time we actually have. After all, time is not elastic. Each of us has the same amount of time each day: 24 hours or 1440 minutes.

How we organize our time often determines how successful we will be, not how much time we actually have.

Of course, when some people hear the word "organize" they immediately start to groan. Who has time to get organized? Anyway, what's wrong with leaving things until the last minute, with always being late, with working in a messy, cluttered space? It's a chore to be organized.

Stephanie Winston, author of the best-selling book *Getting Organized: The Easy Way to Put Your Life in Order,* disagrees. "Organizing is fun, really," she says. What's more, it puts you "in charge of your world." As this book shows you, organizing your time and your work teaches you to:

- prioritize
- be on time
- have more time
- reduce stress
- be more selective

Prioritize

Brian Beaudin is senior vice president for a business and industry association that sponsors programs in time management. One of the problems with time management, as he sees it, is that employees often don't know which project should have the highest priority. "They start six things," he explains, "and don't finish any of them. They say, 'Oh, I think I'll start this letter.' Then they stop in the middle to make a phone call. Instead of going back to the letter, they say 'I have this report due,' and they begin the report. By the end of the day, nothing gets completed."

Effective time management ensures that this doesn't happen to you. It teaches you how to set priorities,

---

EXERCISE

If you want to succeed in the workplace, you need to learn new skills constantly so you can get more accomplished. Write about a new skill that you recently acquired on your job or in an extracurricular activity. How did you feel about being able to master this skill? How has learning this skill helped you accomplish more? Think about which skill you should learn next.

how to determine which tasks are most important, and how to make sure those tasks get done. How critical are these skills on a job? A recent advertisement for an editorial assistant position at a major publishing company sought candidates that have "the ability to work on and prioritize many projects at once." Thus, an editorial assistant is expected to keep many balls in the air at the same time and make sure none of them fall. This takes organization skills.

Melissa Gomez is an administrator at a small manufacturing company. Melissa describes her job as "organized chaos," with emphasis on the word "organized." Melissa is expected to write proposals for a variety of government jobs on which her company is bidding. Each proposal must be submitted by a specific deadline. If the proposal is late, her company will lose the project. Therefore, careful time management is essential in her position.

Do not squander time, for that is the stuff life is made of.

—Benjamin Franklin, American scientist,
statesman, and diplomat

Be on Time

"In school you can be absent or late, and everything can be worked out," says career counselor Phyllis Garrison. "But the real world is different." Garrison says she gets feedback from employers that some students aren't responsible. The students don't "show up every day on time. Kids who are successful allow enough time for everything." Adds college senior Rachel Anderson, "I think being on time is just an assumption that employers make. It's part of the job."

While still in high school, Anderson participated in a unique field-study program. Students developed a list of businesses that might be interested in offering internships. They created a concise interview guide to determine what types of internships might be developed. Then they contacted the organizations, interviewed key individuals, and analyzed the data. Finally, they wrote reports describing the internships, together with a plan to implement the program at their school.

"This project exercised the skills of time management," explains Charles Jett, who helped design the project. "If you put off one step, then you can't proceed to the next one," he points out. Jett adds that if students left the task of collecting data until the last minute, they wouldn't have enough time to analyze it properly or write an effective report. The moral is simple: Whenever you're involved in a team project, it's important to do each part of the project promptly. This takes time-management skills.

Have More Time

Some people think that organizing activities takes too much time. But, in fact, it gives you more time. "You probably don't realize it," writes Jeffrey Mayer in his book *Time Management For Dummies*, "but most people waste almost an hour a day looking for papers that are lost on the tops of their desks—60 percent of which they don't need anyway." (Chapter 5 describes how to make your work space more user-friendly so you can get more done in less time.)

By organizing your time, you're also more likely to remain focused on the most important things that have to be accomplished each day. This helps you avoid distractions. Once your priorities are accomplished, you have more time to relax.

EXERCISE

Describe the last time that you completed a project late or arrived late for something, such as a class or part-time job.

- How did you feel about being late?

- Why were you late?

- Did you offer an excuse for being late? If so, what was it?

- What was the reaction of the person to whom you offered the excuse?

- How did your tardiness affect other people?

- Why is it important to be on time?

- List three things you can do to be on time from now on.

FACT

In business, as much as 50–70 percent of the day is wasted on unimportant tasks like meeting with unexpected visitors and answering telephone calls.

Reduce Stress

"Some people like living on the edge, but I don't," explains Rachel Anderson. "I find it very stressful to leave something until the last minute. I don't complete it as well." Anderson described a paper that she waited too long to begin. She needed time to finish a rough draft, put it away, and go back to it in a few days to edit the paper effectively. But she didn't leave herself enough time. Then her computer broke down at the last minute, and she had to scurry around to find another one. This just added to her stress.

Murphy's Law states: Anything that can go wrong will go wrong.

Murphy's Law states: Anything that can go wrong will go wrong. This law is generally in effect whenever something is left until the last minute. For example, you put off that big paper until the night before it is due; then your computer breaks or the printer doesn't work. You wait until the last possible second to leave for a job interview; then you get stuck in traffic and arrive late. You decide to pull an all-nighter to finish that science project; then you come down with the flu and can't get out of bed. By organizing your time, these kinds of problems can often be avoided.

Be More Selective

"Time management gives you an effective way of learning to say no," explains Charles Jett. "You know you don't have time to do everything."

Peter Burns, a college senior, explains that he is involved in a variety of campus activities, perhaps too many activities. He works part time, serves as president of his class, and tries to handle a full academic load. "I'd come home and there would be 15 messages on my answering machine," he explains. Burns says that he tries to get several important priorities accomplished each day but that he never gets everything done. "I've had to be selective. I've begun to say no to opportunities. Academics are more important than extracurricular activities."

Time is the most valuable thing that a man can spend.

—Theophrastis, Greek philosopher

Time management is a way of giving yourself more control over your life. Instead of simply being reactive—responding to the messages on your answering machine or the requests of your friends—you can be proactive. Ask yourself: "What is most important to me?" The answer to this question can enable you to set priorities and establish goals.

In his book, *The 7 Habits of Highly Effective People*, Stephen Covey writes: "The challenge is not to manage time, but to manage ourselves." This means saying "no" to what is not important and saying "yes" to what is.

TIME TO ORGANIZE

Two centuries ago, farmers told time by observing the position of the sun. They organized their work by the seasons of the year—sowing in the spring, harvesting in the fall. If their schedule was off by a day or an

This advertising executive stays organized by maintaining a clean workspace and prioritizing his activities. (Corbis)

hour, it didn't make too much difference. But with the rise of the factory system, notions of time and work changed. Large numbers of employees had to be organized to manufacture products. This meant that their work had to be timed precisely by the clock. All of them started their jobs at the same time, worked together as a team throughout the day, and finished when the factory whistle blew. Thus, time management became an essential part of the workplace.

The most successful almanacs made time management their explicit focus, and of these [the] . . . Old Farmer's Almanac, by the middle of the nineteenth century had become the model for imitators all over the country.

—Michael O'Malley in *Keeping Watch, A History of American Time*

Today, time management is more important than ever before. Corporate downsizings have reduced the number of employees in every organization. Those who still have jobs are often expected to do more work in the same amount of time. What's more, they are required to master not only one job, but often a variety of different jobs. In light of these changes, effective time management is a critical skill for career success. It enables you to focus on and accomplish

───────── EXERCISE ─────────

Do you organize your time and your life effectively? You can't improve your organization skills until you pinpoint which areas of your life need work. Answer true or false to the following statements. If your answer makes you realize that you have a time-management conflict in your life, ask yourself what you might do to change your behavior.

- I set priorities for myself each day, each week, each month.

- At the end of each day, I generally feel that I accomplished something important.

- I am easily distracted from doing my work.

- I usually feel stressed out because I have too much to do.

- I use a schedule that helps me plan my time.

- I arrive late for appointments.

- I keep my workspace neat so I can find everything easily.

- I clutter up my computer with unnecessary files.

- I procrastinate and leave assignments until the last minute.

the most important priorities, teaches you the value of being on time, and reduces the stress associated with being late. Finally, spending a little time to organize your work can actually buy you more time.

The process of organizing your time and your life should begin now, even before you've started a career. In school or a part-time job, you have an opportunity to experiment—to learn what works for you and what doesn't. With this knowledge, you're far more likely to be an outstanding performer when you embark on a career.

IN SUMMARY . . .

■ Organizing time effectively is a critical skill for anyone who wants to succeed in the workplace.

■ Five changes take place when you organize your time and your work:

- You put first things first.

- You learn to be on time.

- You have more time.

- You reduce stress.

- You learn to be more selective.

- Work schedules have changed ever since the rise of the factory system in the early 1800s. Time management has become a critical part of the day-to-day management of individual jobs and the workings of large organizations.

- Downsizing has reduced the number of employees in every organization, so today's employees are expected to do more than ever.

- In order to improve your organization skills, you must first pinpoint which areas of your life are the least organized. (For example, is your cluttered desk your main concern, or are your time-management skills your biggest organizational problem?)

- When you start to reorganize, don't forget to factor in Murphy's Law, which states: Anything that can go wrong will go wrong.

- Although organizing activities takes time, it will actually leave you with more time in the long run.

2

MANAGING YOUR SCHEDULE

J anet had recently joined her school's service club. Members of the club volunteered their time, delivering hot meals to elderly shut-ins, staffing a hotline at the community crisis center, and doing other types of service work. Each year the group also sponsored an auction to raise money for various community programs, such as a homeless shelter and a soup kitchen.

"As you all know," the president of the club began, "we're already receiving items to sell at the auction. But we have to make sure everybody in town knows about it. Since John Thompson graduated last year, there's no one to handle publicity. Are there any volunteers?"

As the club president asked this question, he was looking directly at Janet. She had always done well in English and had even won a school writing prize. "How about it, Janet, would you take on the job? You're the best qualified." She smiled and nodded her head.

"Thanks, it's very important," the club president said. "There are only two newspapers in town. Please find out their deadlines so you can be sure to get the stories in on time. We can't afford to be late."

Janet made a note on a small piece of paper and tucked it inside one of her notebooks and made a mental note to call as soon as possible. But that afternoon, she had to go to her part-time job at the supermarket and forgot to contact the newspapers. Several days went by, and Janet became involved in other activities. She had to finish her science project and study for final exams. There were applications to complete for college. About 10 days before the date of the auction, Janet sat down to write the articles for the local newspapers. It still seemed like plenty of time to her, but as she opened one of her notebooks to jot down a few ideas, a little piece of paper fell out. It was the reminder to check the deadlines at the papers.

"Well, there's nothing I can do about it now," she thought. "I'll just finish these articles as fast as I can and get them into the papers." A couple of days later, Janet completed her final drafts and hurried down to one of the newspapers after school. She located the editorial office and gave the article to an editor. But as he looked at the date of the auction, he shook his head. "I'm sorry," he said, "our deadline for this type of article closed four days ago. You're too late."

Janet couldn't believe it. "But there must be something you can do," she said.

"I'm afraid not," he told her. "There's just no room for it."

She left the office in a panic. She decided to call the other newspaper from a pay phone in the hallway. "The deadline has already passed," the editor told her. "But, maybe we can run a paragraph or two."

"No one will ever see it," she shot back.

"I'm sorry," he explained, "it's really the best we can do."

Janet hung up the telephone. "How could I let this happen?" she asked herself. "What will I tell the other club members?"

BUSY, BUSY, BUSY

Regardless of whether it's business or pleasure, one rule holds true for today's society: We seem to thrive on being busy. There are always projects to do, meetings to attend, assignments to complete, phone calls to answer, people to see, and email to read. But being busy doesn't always mean that your most significant tasks are being accomplished. Take Janet, for example. She let a critical deadline slip, jeopardizing the success of the auction.

Being busy doesn't always mean that your most significant tasks are being accomplished.

How often do you look back at the end of a week and ask yourself: Did I accomplish everything that was really important? Did I forget to do something that I should have done? Did I waste time on

FOUR KEY STEPS IN ORGANIZING YOUR TIME

1. Determine how you spend your time now.

2. Make a to-do list.

3. Prioritize your activities.

4. Put those activities on a weekly schedule.

unimportant things? These questions will help you recognize your weaknesses and avoid the type of problem that Janet encountered. You will learn to use time more efficiently.

WHAT IS QUALITY?

- Eliminating mistakes.
- Doing things right the first time.
- Giving employers, customers, and teachers what they ask for.
- Finishing projects on time.

WHERE DOES THE TIME GO?

If you go to work in any major company, you'll hear a great deal about quality. Customers demand high-quality products. In order to meet this demand, major corporations have embarked on extensive programs aimed at improving the quality of their products and services, as well as the inner workings of their various departments.

How does a company know if it's making improvements? Quality-control managers begin with what they call a "baseline." They look at the current number of defects in their products, such as copy machines or automobiles. Then they set goals for improvement. After a certain length of time, they evaluate the company's progress to see if the goals are being met.

You can use a similar approach to improve the way you organize your time. Begin by looking at the way you use your time today. This is your baseline. By evaluating how your time is currently being spent, you may begin to realize why some of your most important projects are not being accomplished. Or you may start to understand why you're always finishing them late.

MAKE A TO-DO LIST

"I make a to-do list, otherwise I forget things," explains career counselor Carol Peterson. "I have

————— EXERCISE —————

Keep a log for a week on how you use your time. This is your baseline. At the end of each day, write down:

ACTIVITY	AMOUNT OF TIME
1. Classes	____
2. Study halls	____
3. Extracurricular activities	____
4. Talking on the telephone	____
5. Watching television	____
6. Homework assignments	____
7. Hanging out with friends	____
8. Part-time job	____
9. Hanging out with your family	____
10. Relaxing	____
11. Cleaning or doing laundry	____
12. Sleeping	____

pads of paper in every room. As I think of things, I write them down. Then I put all of them on a central list." For example, if Janet had put the note to call the newspapers and check the deadlines on a central list, she might not have forgotten to do it.

Consider another example of the importance of to-do lists. Jose works for a small publishing company. Each week, there are meetings to attend and important telephone calls to make. There are manuscripts to review, pictures to approve, and project reports to complete.

Unfortunately, Jose isn't on top of his hectic schedule. It's not that he procrastinates—in fact, he is a very conscientious worker. However, each time there is a new task for him to do, he writes it on a little slip of paper and puts it in some part of his office. His office is covered with these little notes. Often, one is tacked on top of another. Jose has no central to-do list with everything on it. As a result, calls go unanswered and he sometimes forgets important meetings.

Be sure there is at least one place where all the items can be found and checked off . . . keep it current and make sure it's available to you at all times.

—B. Eugene Griessman in *Time Tactics of Very Successful People*

In order to avoid the pitfalls of Jose's disorganized system of many notes, make a to-do list at the beginning of each week. If you're a student, your list might include homework assignments that are due during the week, quizzes and tests, and club meetings. In addition, you can use your to-do list to write down important errands, such as picking up food for your cat or remembering to change the tires on your car.

SUGGESTIONS FOR YOUR TO-DO LIST

Maintain order in your life by putting even errands and small tasks such as these in writing.

- Pick up a prescription
- Get a haircut
- Attend doctor, dentist, and other appointments
- Pay the bills
- Get the oil changed in the car
- Wash the car
- Buy groceries
- Clean the house
- Do laundry

MAKING LITTLE TASKS OUT OF BIG TASKS

Sometimes you're given long-term assignments such as a research paper or science project. Instead of leaving these assignments until the last minute, break down each task into its logical steps. Then you can put the steps on your to-do list and complete them, one after the other. High school counselor Angela Martinez tells students to "always write things down; otherwise they'll forget them. I tell college-bound students that professors won't plan for you. They'll just say that a paper is due on a specific date, and you have to create your own mini-deadlines for completing each part of it so you'll finish on time." In other words, set realistic deadlines for all of the little tasks that one major assignment entails.

Break down each task into its logical steps.

For example, perhaps you're assigned to write an article that's due in three weeks for the school newspaper. On your to-do list for the first week, you might put: "Conduct interviews and do research." For the next week, you might enter: "Write rough draft." And for the third week, you might write: "Revise rough draft and edit." By working backward from your deadline, you can determine what has to be accomplished each week to finish the task comfortably and on time.

Suppose you've decided to obtain a part-time job. On your to-do list for the first week, you might put: "Write resume." For the second week, you might

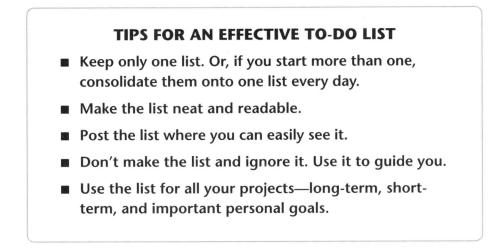

TIPS FOR AN EFFECTIVE TO-DO LIST

■ Keep only one list. Or, if you start more than one, consolidate them onto one list every day.

■ Make the list neat and readable.

■ Post the list where you can easily see it.

■ Don't make the list and ignore it. Use it to guide you.

■ Use the list for all your projects—long-term, short-term, and important personal goals.

assign yourself the task of identifying businesses in your area that are looking for part-time employees. For the third week, you might decide to call those businesses and make appointments with the ones who want to interview you. Subdividing your activities in this way will make your goals seem less daunting and more realistic.

DON'T FORGET LONG-TERM GOALS

Frequently, the days and weeks seem to be filled with projects that demand our immediate attention. In his book *The 7 Habits of Highly Effective People*,

Stephen Covey points out that many of us seem to have very little time to focus on long-term goals. As a result, we can often miss out on unusual opportunities that may allow us to grow as individuals. But these things also belong on our to-do lists—that's if we ever expect to fulfill our potential as unique human beings.

Julie worked for a large telemarketing firm. One day she hoped to be part of management. In order to reach this goal, she knew that there were a number of steps she had to take along the way. There were training courses that she needed to attend in team building, communications, and leadership. She volunteered for special projects that would expand her knowledge and develop her skills as a manager. Each

EXERCISE

Make a to-do list for the week. Include short- and long-term assignments, errands, and extracurricular activities. Break down the long-term projects into separate steps and include the initial step on this week's to-do list. Also make sure to include an important goal you would like to achieve and the first step you might take toward accomplishing it.

week, Julie's work in her training courses and on special projects formed important elements of her to-do list.

SET PRIORITIES

Jamie is assistant manager of the human resources department at a small electronics firm. It's a two-person department, so she and her boss are constantly busy. Each week, Jamie makes a to-do list of the tasks she wants to accomplish. Then she breaks down the list and establishes the top-priority items that she wants to have done by the end of each day. This is how Jamie ensures that her highest priorities are always accomplished.

On Tuesday, for example, Jamie must finish preparing a presentation she has to make to top management the following day. In addition, she wants to begin planning a summer internship program with a local community college. Jamie also wants to schedule a meeting with company supervisors to talk about sexual harassment guidelines for employees. Finally, she must complete the final draft of a new employee handbook that has to be on the president's desk by Thursday morning. And Jamie has to be out of the office all day Wednesday, so she won't have time to work on the handbook.

Jamie believes that she can accomplish all of these tasks—that is, if nothing unexpected occurs that demands her immediate attention. But in the workplace, crises often seem to occur when they're least expected. On Tuesday morning the firm's receptionist walks into Jamie's office and suddenly announces that she is quitting.

Jamie meets her boss, the human resources manager, and together they decide how to handle the situation. Jamie calls an employment agency that supplies temporary workers. The agency agrees to send over several job candidates who can fill the position for the short term. Jamie spends part of the afternoon interviewing three candidates. She also prepares a newspaper advertisement announcing a receptionist opening. Jamie and her boss review the copy for the ad and send it to the newspaper.

By the time Jamie has finished handling the crisis, Tuesday has almost ended. None of her priorities have been accomplished. She can put off planning the new internship program and scheduling the meeting on sexual harassment guidelines. But the benefits presentation and the employment manual must be finished. Jamie stays late until both projects are finally complete.

Setting priorities is an important element of organizing your time and work. This is the best way to ensure that the most important items on your to-do list get done each day. Of course, no one has complete control over his or her time. Unexpected events are always occurring, and you have to adjust your day to deal with them. Perhaps you can put off some of your priorities the way Jamie did. But others must be accomplished. If you put your priorities in writing, you can go back to them after a crisis has passed. And even if it means working late, you can accomplish your most important priorities every day.

Once you determine what your priorities are, get a start on each project. Don't neglect unpleasant tasks—you will have to do them sooner or later. Decide which tasks absolutely have to be finished first; then set small deadlines for different parts of them. This way, if a crisis occurs, you can refer to your organized list to see exactly what order the tasks should be completed in.

❖ ❖ ❖

William is a high school senior with a busy schedule. He has classes and homework each day, as well as a part-time job at the public library. Sunday night, before the week begins, William writes a to-do list. Then he selects the tasks that are his important priorities for each day of the week. William realizes that some of these priorities might change as he gets new assignments in school. Some of these assignments may become top priorities, and other tasks on his list may have to be postponed.

William's to-do list for Tuesday and the priorities he has set for himself are shown below. His most important priorities have a (1) beside them, and lesser priorities have a (2).

WILLIAM'S TO-DO LIST FOR TUESDAY

Finish final draft of English paper	(1)
Start research for science project	(2)
Buy birthday gift for Dad	(2)
Do math homework	(1)
Meet friends at ice-skating rink	(2)
Work at library (4:00–6:00 P.M.)	(1)

William must finish his English paper because it is due on Wednesday. He always has a math assignment. This must be completed before the next class, which is the following morning. He also has to work at the library. The other tasks are things he would like to do, but are not absolutely essential. His father's birthday, for example, is not until the following Monday, so he could postpone this task if necessary.

While William is sitting in history class on Tuesday, the teacher announces an unexpected quiz for the next day. This quiz now becomes one of his top priorities on the to-do list. To have time enough to study for the quiz and still complete the other essential tasks on his list, William may need to postpone all of his lesser priorities.

By prioritizing each day's projects, William is assured of accomplishing those that are most important—even if it means spending some extra time studying for a quiz.

EXERCISE

■ Return to your weekly to-do list. Break down the list into tasks that you want to accomplish each day. Place a (1) next to the most important priorities; place a (2) next to less important priorities.

■ Suppose your teacher gives you a new assignment on Tuesday that must be completed by the following day. How will this affect your list of priorities for that day? Suppose your car breaks down on Thursday while you're driving to work. How will this affect your priorities for that day?

DEVELOP A SCHEDULE

Once you have determined how you spend your time, made a to-do list, and set your priorities. The next step toward managing your time is to develop a weekly schedule, broken down day by day. "Some young people use planners," explains high school counselor Phyllis Garrison, "and this gives them a structured approach to everything."

Develop a weekly schedule, broken down day by day.

A planner includes each day of the week, and it often divides the days into hours. First you can block out the time you spend in class. Then you can add the priority items from your to-do list. William's schedule for Tuesday is shown on the next page.

William has four hours of classes on Monday. If you recall, his math homework was a top priority, so he schedules it for his study hall at 11:00 A.M. William had hoped to meet some friends at the ice-skating rink, but his history teacher announced an unexpected quiz for the following day. Therefore, he decided to stay at school and complete his math homework so he would have time at night to study for the quiz. On his schedule, William includes two other important priorities: working at the library and finishing his English paper. He had also hoped to start his science project. But he had to change his schedule and study for the history quiz instead.

Although William's schedule is busy, he still leaves himself sufficient time between various activities.

WILLIAM'S SCHEDULE FOR TUESDAY

9:00–10:00 A.M.	English class
10:00–11:00 A.M.	Biology class
11:00–12:00 P.M.	Study hall: Start math homework
12:00–12:30 P.M.	Lunch
12:30–1:30 P.M.	History class
1:30–2:30 P.M.	Sociology class
2:30–3:30 P.M.	Meet friends at ice-skating rink
4:00–6:00 P.M.	Work at library
6:30–7:00 P.M.	Dinner
7:30–9:00 P.M.	Finish English paper
9:30–10:30 P.M.	Start science project

Breaks give you a chance to refresh yourself so you can do your work more effectively.

"Some students don't leave themselves enough time to get from one place to another," says Peterson, "like getting from school to a part-time job." William allows half an hour, more than enough time, to drive to and from his job at the library. He also builds in free time during the evening to take breaks. Breaks are an important part of any schedule. You can use them to have a snack, watch television, or call friends. Breaks give you a chance to refresh yourself so you can do your work more effectively.

Another way to keep track of your schedule is via computer accessories. Handheld computer devices, such as a personal digital assistant (PDA) like the Palm Pilot, are excellent for organizing your daily and weekly activities. Portable devices such as this enable you to make note of changes or additions to your schedule whether you are in your office or on a walk during your lunch hour. Computer organizers can be used to take notes in meetings as well as store digital photos, audio books, and other applications. They also allow you to keep phone numbers and addresses on hand. In addition, handheld computer devices allow you to download news and weather, spreadsheets, databases, medical and financial calculators, and many other useful pieces of information.

You may also wish to keep track of your schedule with help

Workers today are constantly on the go. To stay organized when you are busy, create a schedule and stick to it. (Corbis)

——— EXERCISE ———

Create a weekly schedule, broken down day by day. Use the information from your to-do list and your daily list of priorities. Block out your classes. Include any extracurricular activities or part-time jobs. Be sure to leave enough time for travel and breaks.

---

from computer software programs. Programs such as Microsoft Outlook help with personal-information management. Outlook helps you to manage multiple email accounts, sends you email reminders, and performs other organizational tasks.

MANAGE YOUR WAY TO SUCCESS

Managing your time and your work is a step-by-step process. It begins by taking stock of where you are now. Ask yourself: How do I currently spend my time? How many of my important priorities are really being accomplished? Would I be more successful in school and in the rest of my life if I spent my time differently?

Make yourself a to-do list at the beginning of each week. As new projects come along, add them to your list. We rarely have time to do everything on our to-do lists, so it's essential to set some priorities for yourself and decide the most important things you must do every day. Finally, make a schedule that enables you to carry out the high-priority tasks on your list. You'll be delighted to discover how much more productive you become.

MY TO-DO LIST

My goal this week is to: _____

Task	Priority	Deadline	Completed

IN SUMMARY . . .

- Quality work means giving employers and teachers what they ask for on time and without mistakes.

- Managing your time and work is a step-by-step process. The four key steps to organizing your time are:

  - Determine how you currently spend your time.

  - Make a to-do list.

  - Prioritize your activities.

  - Make a weekly schedule for these activities.

- Keep only one to-do list that is neat and easy to read. Post the list where it will be easily seen, and use it for errands and assignments as well as for long-term and short-term goals.

- Develop a weekly schedule by dividing each day into increments (half-hour or hour increments work best).

3

ELIMINATING
TIME WASTERS

Michelle was supposed to be studying for a science test. It was an important exam that counted heavily toward her final grade, but she just couldn't seem to get down to work.

First there was a telephone call from her friend Arlene, complaining about her boss again. "I don't know what to do," Arlene began. "My boss is so unfair. He doesn't care about anybody." It was 45 minutes later before Arlene finally stopped talking and Michelle put down the telephone.

Michelle had no sooner gone back to studying for the test when the doorbell rang. It was her friend Karen from across the street. "You'll never believe what happened," she told Michelle. Karen had the latest gossip about their friends Bill and Carol who had just broken up. It took her at least an hour and two cups of coffee to pour out the entire story. Then it was time for Michelle's favorite television program, so Karen stayed to watch it with her. By the time Karen left, it was 10:00 P.M.

"I've really got to start studying," Michelle told herself. But first she decided to check her email. There was a short letter from her brother who was away at college. She decided to answer it.

Finally, Michelle opened her chemistry notes. She looked at the clock—11:00 P.M. The exam was scheduled for first period the next morning, and Michelle hadn't even begun preparing for it.

TERRIBLE TIME WASTERS

Michelle is no different from many of us. She wants to get her work done. Indeed, she may have even reserved a large block of time in her schedule to study for the chemistry test. But somehow she finds herself getting distracted by interruptions. After all, what's more enjoyable? Talking to your friends or reviewing your science notes?

Learn to say no like a maniac to your time wasters.

**—Helen Gurley Brown, author and former
editor of *Cosmopolitan* magazine**

Unfortunately, time wasters prevent you from completing your most essential priorities. Whether it's a school assignment or a project at work, you can't afford to let a critical task go undone because of unimportant distractions.

MANAGE TELEPHONE CALLS

The telephone can be one of your biggest distractions. Unless you learn to control the phone, it will surely master you. There is something about the insistent "ring-ring" of the telephone that demands our attention. Whenever we hear that sound, our tendency is to stop whatever we're doing—no matter how necessary it may be—and immediately answer the call. We simply must find out what the caller has to say to us, even if it means interrupting something else. So we pick up the telephone and put the rest of our schedule on hold.

Telephone messages generally can be grouped into three categories: essential, time-limited, and unimportant calls.

The telephone can be one of your biggest distractions. Unless you learn to control the phone, it will surely master you.

Essential Calls
Essential calls require your immediate attention. You might receive a call from your boss who needs to discuss a critical presentation that you're making at

tomorrow's sales conference. Or perhaps you receive a call from a customer who wants you to find out why a shipment is late. Essential calls are ones that you must answer, spending as much time as it takes to handle them properly.

FACT

The average business call lasts six minutes but can actually be concluded in two minutes.

Time-Limit Calls

Time-limit calls may be important, but they should be handled as quickly and efficiently as possible. For example, a member of your work team may call with a specific question about a report you're working on together. You answer it in about a minute. Then he spends the next 20 minutes talking about his recent vacation. This is a real time waster that can delay high-priority work. It's essential to put a limit on these types of calls; otherwise you'll find yourself frittering away precious minutes. If your coworker wants to talk about his vacation and you have a project to accomplish, you don't have to cut him off rudely. Explain the situation as pleasantly as possible: "I'm sorry, but I really have to get this done. Can I call you back later or see you for lunch? I'd love to hear about

TELEPHONE ETIQUETTE
IN BUSINESS SITUATIONS

According to experts at The Telephone Doctor, a telephone-etiquette company, there are guidelines to follow when answering the phone at work:

- Answer in a professional manner. Follow the standard answering procedure of the company, which may include stating the company name followed by your name.

- Put a caller on hold if you have to speak to someone else in the office. If a caller hears you speaking to someone else, you'll come off as distracted and unprofessional.

- Do not type emails while you are on the telephone at work—the caller will likely be able to hear the typing.

- Speak clearly and in an upbeat manner. Slang or casual words such as "yeah" and "uh-huh" are not appropriate in a business setting.

- Maintain a service-oriented attitude when you speak on the telephone.

- Avoid joking. When you can't see the caller's face, it is difficult to gauge a reaction.

Source: *Chicago Tribune*

your vacation." Make an appointment to call him, if necessary, and mark it down on your schedule.

Unimportant Calls

"Unimportant" here means unimportant compared with the work you really need to accomplish. Michelle's call from Arlene falls into this category. Michelle should have been studying instead of spending 45 minutes listening to Arlene's complaints about her boss. But perhaps Michelle is one of those people who simply has trouble saying no. She's afraid of offending her friends, so Michelle finds herself listening to their telephone monologues instead of focusing on her school priority.

One high-school senior explains that when she's involved in an important assignment, she simply tells friends who call that she will have to speak to them later. She is nice but firm. This senior seems to have no trouble saying no or dealing with her high-priority tasks *before* she spends time on the telephone.

If saying no is more of a problem for you, perhaps you should consider using an answering machine. This is an effective way to screen calls and decide whether you want to answer them. Businesses and some individuals often use voice mail—a central computerized phone-messaging system—instead of traditional answering machines for this same purpose. It's important to have an outgoing message that's short, friendly, and encourages callers to talk. For example, you might say: "I'm sorry I can't take your call right now. But, after the beep, please leave a message. I'll get back to you as soon as I can." This way you won't miss their message, and you won't be forced to tell them "no" when they want to talk to you.

You'll also find that many of your calls do not have to be returned. Frequently, a caller is just providing you with information that requires no response. Perhaps a customer is calling to say he can't make tomorrow's luncheon appointment, or a coworker is leaving you some statistical data. This type of message usually does not require a return call from you.

You might also consider using email as a way of avoiding interruptions while doing homework. Suggest that friends use an instant messaging program (IM) or email to contact you. At various intervals throughout the evening, take a break from homework to check your email or IM program. If anything seems important, take a few minutes to get back to your friends, and then sign off of your computer and return to work.

Cell Phone Calls
As a real estate agent, Darlene was constantly working in different locations. She depended on the cell phone her boss had given her as a way to stay in contact with her clients, her boss, and her coworkers. However, Darlene decided that she would use the same cell phone for both work and personal calls. She was often showing a property to potential buyers and

was interrupted by unimportant calls from her friends. Since she had to leave her cell phone on during work hours in case her boss called, Darlene became frustrated by the interruptions that the personal calls made to her presentations. Darlene's business reputation suffered as clients noticed that she often seemed distracted. Finally, Darlene realized that her business life and her personal life had to be separated if she was ever going to succeed, so she purchased her own cell phone and used it only outside of business hours for personal calls.

Cell-phone usage can be very time-consuming. If you work out of multiple locations or sites, it may be necessary for you to keep your cell phone turned on during work hours. If this is the case, let your friends and family know that during work hours your cell phone number is only for emergencies. Or, if possible, use two different cell phones for work and personal calls. If you know you'll be receiving work-related calls on your cell phone, be sure to leave an away message that is appropriate, friendly, and professional. Don't get carried away with checking your personal messages during work hours.

FACT

Approximately 50 percent of all telephone calls are simply conveying information that requires no response.

EXERCISE

Telephone calls can be terrible time wasters. Keep a log of your calls for a week and mark each call as one of the following:

- essential

- time limit

- unimportant

Indicate how much time you spend on each call. Finally, decide what steps you could have taken to cut down your telephone time.

TALK, TALK, TALK

It used to be that the water cooler was the symbol of gossip in corporate America. Newspaper and magazine cartoons showed employees standing around the water cooler trading the latest news. This is not the case anymore. Because of corporate downsizings, there are far fewer employees in every organization. That means everyone has more work to do and there's very little time to stand around the water cooler and talk. What's more, any employees seen wasting time are apt to be looking for new jobs soon.

Because of corporate downsizings, there are far fewer employees in every organization.

Teyonda Riley works after school at a fast-food restaurant. She knows that the restaurant manager expects her to be standing behind the cash register, waiting on customers all the time she's there. If her friends come in and want to talk, Teyonda makes it clear that she has no time to spend with them. "Business comes first," she says.

When you're trying to get work done, management experts suggest that you prioritize conversations just as you do telephone calls. Some conversations are essential, others are unimportant, and still others must be time limited. Career counselor Carol Peterson must juggle a variety of tasks in her job. She calls employers, trying to find part-time jobs for students.

TYPES OF TIME WASTERS

- Needless telephone conversations
- Useless chit-chat
- Unnecessary interruptions by coworkers
- Poor planning in doing errands
- Unnecessary Internet surfing
- Casual or personal emailing
- Jumping from task to task

She also talks to students, helping them with resumes, job searches, and interviewing strategies.

Peterson's conversations with students are *essential*, because they depend on her for information. The conversations Teyonda Riley described are *unimportant*, so she wisely avoids them. But you will probably find that many of your conversations at work are *time limited*. And it's necessary to learn how to handle them or you won't get your high-priority tasks accomplished.

One approach is to answer brief questions politely but to put off more complicated ones until you have more time. Suppose you're in the midst of an important project, and a coworker stops to ask you a question. "We just received a shipment from Acme Lighting. Do you know where the shipping order is?" If you know the answer, you can stop and quickly answer the question.

But suppose your coworker wants to continue the discussion. "You know, I've been meaning to mention something. I think we need to improve our order forms." At this point, you realize that the topic might lead to a long conversation that will interrupt your work. You might say: "I'm sorry. I know this may be important to you. But I can't stop right now. Why don't I call you later and we can talk about it then." This enables you to have a brief conversation without taking much time away from your project.

Another way of dealing with the same situation is to suggest that your coworker speak to someone else about the new order forms. You can point out that this person might be more knowledgeable on the subject than you are. Finally, you might encourage your coworker to do some research on his own. He could find out what kinds of forms other companies use and perhaps even design one of his own. Then he might come back and talk about it.

Each of these approaches enables you to set a time limit on conversations and keep yourself focused on the important work that has to be done each day.

AVOID OVERUSING THE INTERNET

The Internet has revolutionized the way that we do business today. It houses an enormous variety of information, and its availability has significantly reduced production times around the world. However, if you have access to the Internet at work, keep in mind that it is not for personal use. Checking the latest news or reading about a local event online can waste time and make you lose focus. In fact, your employer may monitor all Internet activity within your office to ensure that it is used solely for business purposes, so it is best not to engage in Internet surfing while on the job. To save time when you do use the Internet for work purposes, bookmark websites that you frequently use on the job.

Email is another example of a time waster. Sorting through emails can be quite time-consuming, as this has become a very popular form of communication—almost as popular as the telephone. Be sure to have separate email accounts for business matters and personal matters, so you don't have to spend time sorting them out at work. Delete all old or unimportant emails in a timely fashion so that you don't build up an unorganized stack of messages and clutter up your mailbox.

Jumping from task to task in an unorganized manner can also waste time. If you barely make a dent in one project before starting the next, it will be difficult to ever make real progress. To avoid falling into this trap, make yourself stay on a project for a specified amount of time (for example, at least one or two hours) before moving on to the next.

WHAT CONSTITUTES AN ESSENTIAL CONVERSATION?

- An emergency that can't wait.

- Your boss needing speak to you immediately.

- The school principal wanting you in his or her office.

- A friend or family member depending on you for help.

- A coworker who can't complete a project without some essential information that you possess.

────── **EXERCISE** ──────

Keep track of those conversations that occur during the day that distract you from your work. How many of them were unimportant? How many could have been much shorter? How can you shorten them next time?

MORE TIME WASTERS

Linda saved Saturdays to do her errands. She made a mental list of what she had to accomplish and set out to get everything done, but she always complained that she never had enough time.

Linda's typical Saturday is quite busy. She drives to one part of town to drop off her dry cleaning. Then she retraces her route to shop at a children's clothing store near her house. Linda wants to buy a birthday gift for her one-year-old niece. No sooner has she completed this purchase than she realizes that she needs to go to the bank to deposit her paycheck. But it's next door to the cleaners, so she drives over there again.

By now, it's lunchtime and Linda returns home. During lunch she realizes that she has forgotten something else on her shopping trip—a birthday card to go with the present for her niece. The card shop is only a block from the children's clothing store, so after lunch she retraces her steps to that part of town. Then Linda has to do some grocery shopping. Guess what? The supermarket is next to the bank. By the end of the day, Linda feels thoroughly exhausted.

FACT

According to *U.S. News & World Report,* time-saving services, such as professional organizing, are among the fastest growing areas for home-based businesses.

Many people waste time because they don't plan their activities very effectively. Keeping a mental list of what you need to do may not be enough—it's too easy to forget something. Instead, write a list of your errands. Then group those that are in the same geographical area and do them together. This way, you're not spending a lot of needless time driving around.

Smart salespeople use a similar approach when they make calls to customers. A salesperson doesn't make one visit, return to the office, go out again and see another customer in the same area, then return to the office. This wastes too much time. Instead she calls ahead, sets up appointments, and tries to see all her customers in the same area on the same day. This cuts down the amount of time she has to spend in traffic.

Many people waste time because they don't plan their activities very effectively.

Make a list of the errands you have to do this week or this weekend. Group those errands that you can do at the same time and in the same physical area. How much time do you save by doing these errands together?

USE SMALL BLOCKS OF TIME

Most of us are forced to spend some time each day traveling to and from work or school. We're also likely to get stuck in traffic. Teacher Anna Gonzalez has learned how to put this time to good use. "My drive to work really makes me think about my day," she says. "I make a mental note of any important telephone calls I need to make at school. Otherwise I forget them or put them off. I also think about any obligation—like a meeting I have to prepare for—and write it down."

Make the most of downtime and in-between time.

—B. Eugene Griessman in *Time Tactics of Very Successful People*

Little blocks of time can be especially valuable if you know how to use them. If you ride to school on the bus in the morning, you can use the time to review your notes before a first-period test. A bus ride to your part-time job is another chance to get some work done—such as a brief reading assignment.

Busy managers know how to use their downtime efficiently. If they travel and their plane is delayed, they bring work to the airport and do it while they're waiting. During this downtime, they might write a letter, read a report, or make telephone calls to customers. A doctor's appointment is another occasion when downtime can be used effectively. Instead of sitting in the waiting room doing nothing, this time can be used to do some work.

WHEN DO YOU DO YOUR BEST WORK?

Each of us has a time of day when we feel freshest and have the most pep. For Anna Gonzalez, that time is the morning. "I have more energy then. That's when I like to schedule important appointments—like meetings with my principal."

Some of us are morning people, which means that's the time when we do our best work. If you're one of these early birds, schedule your hardest tasks—

those that take the most thought—for the morning. Carol Peterson says that she performs at her peak during two times of the day—early morning and early evening. "I do the hardest things then." College senior Peter Burns explains, "I get my best work done before 11:00 P.M. I know that by getting things done then, I won't feel miserable the next morning."

By contrast, time-management experts suggest that you should do less demanding tasks when you have the least amount of energy. In his article, "Time, for a Change," published in *Men's Health,* Richard Laliburte points out that the period between 4:00 and 5:00 P.M. is the least productive part of the workday. Therefore, he recommends that this time be reserved for simple tasks, such as cleaning up your workspace.

——— EXERCISE ———

When do you accomplish your best work? During the next week, keep track of the times when you have the most energy. Is it early in the morning? During the middle of the day? Late afternoon? Evening? Schedule your most difficult tasks during these periods.

TIME WAITS FOR NO ONE

No one can slow down the passing of time, but you can exercise more control over it and increase what you accomplish each day. One way of getting more done is to eliminate those little time wasters. These include some of the lengthy telephone calls and face-to-face conversations that can keep you from doing your work. You can also make better use of your time by designing your schedule to take advantage of your peak energy periods and your down time, as well as by arranging your errands so they can be done most efficiently. These seem like little changes, but you'll be surprised at the difference they can make in your life.

IN SUMMARY . . .

- Know which calls are actually important. There are three types of calls: essential calls, which require immediate attention; time-limit calls, which may be important but should be handled as quickly as possible; and unimportant calls, which require no response.

- Avoid meaningless chit-chat at work. Casual conversation with coworkers is fine, but don't get carried away and end up wasting time.

- Make use of small blocks of time; for example, your commute to work or school or time spent in a doctor's office waiting room are blocks of time that can be used to accomplish tasks.

- Determine when you do your best work. Design your schedule so that you take advantage of key energy times.

- Plan your errands so you don't waste half of your day retracing your steps through the same geographical areas.

- Learn to say no, at least sometimes. To maintain an organized schedule, you will likely have to cut some things out of your schedule.

- Don't let coworkers continually interrupt your work and waste time. Let your coworkers know that you're busy and suggest that they speak to someone else if it's not an emergency.

4

THE PITFALLS OF PROCRASTINATION

Gerry Saunders was a video producer. He created presentations for large companies that they used to sell their new products—anything from baby clothes to cat food. Gerry was considered very talented. Indeed, one of his videos had recently won an award for special effects. Although Gerry was a top-flight producer, he suffered from a terrible problem—procrastination. He always put things off until the last minute.

"I like working on the edge," he said. "It gets my creative juices flowing." But Gerry's procrastination drove his employees to distraction. "One of these days, you're going to cut it too close," his assistant told him.

"Stop worrying," Gerry reassured her. "When have I ever missed a deadline?"

Gerry was currently working on a video presentation for his most important client, a well-known toy manufacturer. They were introducing a new computer game at their annual sales conference. The video was the highlight of the conference and was scheduled to be shown at 10:00 A.M. on the final day, just before the conference ended.

Once again, Gerry had left everything until the last minute. The client, John Fitzgerald, had asked to see a rough cut of the video a couple of days in advance. Gerry had promised to give it to him, but he never delivered. "I really wanted to see the video before we showed it," John explained.

"I'm sorry," Gerry said. "But everything will be all right. Trust me."

"I guess I have no choice," John told him.

With only one day to go before the conference, Gerry worked furiously to finish the videotape. On the last night he never went to bed, and finally at 9:00 A.M.—an hour before show time—the video was complete. Gerry was very proud of what he'd accomplished.

"It's the best work we've ever done," he told his assistant. She nodded her head wearily. Gerry jumped in his car with a copy of the tape and started driving across town to reach the conference by the deadline. Unfortunately, he hadn't counted on traffic. A huge truck had overturned on the highway, and cars were backed up for five miles. There was no way Gerry would reach the conference on time. The deadline came and went, and the videotape was never shown. When Gerry finally arrived, he saw John sitting alone at one end of the auditorium. Everyone else had already gone.

"I'm terribly sorry," Gerry began. "I tried. I really tried. I did the best I could."

"No you didn't," John said angrily. "You always leave everything to the last minute. This time you made me look like a fool. Now I'm going to do what I should have done a long time ago—find another producer."

PROCRASTINATION AND HEALTH

According to a study detailed in the *New York Times,* students who procrastinate get more cold and flu symptoms, more digestive problems, and tend to have unhealthy lifestyles.

The study, conducted by the Procrastination Research Group at Carleton University, found that those who procrastinate also get less sleep and have problems regulating their behavior.

WHY DO PEOPLE PROCRASTINATE?

It's easy to put things off. Suppose you receive an assignment to write a paper. The deadline is several weeks away. "Don't worry," you say to yourself. "There's plenty of time. I can start the assignment later." So you forget about it. Time goes by and you become involved in other things. One day, you remember to look at the calendar. You can't believe it. Suddenly, that deadline is only three days away and you have to work furiously to get your paper done. "Where did the time go?" you ask yourself. Procrastination often seems to make time move more rapidly. By putting off projects, the deadlines appear to sneak up on you almost before you know it.

Procrastination often seems to make time move more rapidly.

Some people, like Gerry Saunders, say they enjoy living on the edge. They just can't focus on a project until the deadline is almost on them. Then they work nonstop—around the clock, if necessary—until the task is accomplished. Some people claim to do their best work that way. But even if they don't, leaving everything until the last minute gives them a convenient excuse. If the project doesn't turn out quite as well as they wanted, they can always say they just ran out of time. It's an easy way to let themselves off the hook, but this does very little for their reputations as reliable workers.

Most of us fall back on procrastination to put off unpleasant tasks—the ones we really don't want to

PROCRASTINATORS' EXCUSES

- "I can always put it off until tomorrow."
- "I do my best work when I'm up against a deadline."
- "I've got more important things to do now."
- "I'm not a procrastinator; I just don't like rushing into anything."
- "If I put it off, maybe the project will go away."
- "If I don't do it, perhaps my boss will forget about it."
- "I want to stop procrastinating, but I don't have time."
- "There's so much to do; I don't know where to start."
- "I don't want to get started too soon."
- "I'll get it done; just don't push me."

do. Instead of starting your math homework, you decide to watch a half hour of television. Then you call a couple of friends on the telephone. Late in the

FOUR REASONS FOR PROCRASTINATION

1. **Perfectionism**, which can create frustration and a reluctance to start projects for fear that they won't be perfect.

2. **Anger/hostility.** If a person is unhappy with a boss or professor, they may delay progress or withhold their own best efforts as a way of "getting even."

3. **Low frustration tolerance.** If someone is overwhelmed by a project, they may feel that it's reasonable to put it off for awhile until your frustration subsides.

4. **Self-deprecation**, or putting down one's own skills, abilities, and accomplishments. If someone does this repeatedly, he or she may eventually come to believe that the are incapable of completing projects and thus put them off.

evening, you finally get around to your homework. By that time you're tired, so you complete only part of it and go to bed.

Sometimes a task may seem so difficult or overwhelming that you don't want to begin. So you put it off. Karen's boss asked her to take some special computer training. But she was afraid the courses might prove too hard for her. Whenever her boss would stop by Karen's desk and inquire if she'd enrolled in the courses, she would say, "Oh, I'll get around to it," but she was afraid to enroll. Karen's fears caused her to procrastinate. But without the necessary training she might eventually lose her job.

Most of us feel anxious when we have to try something new and unfamiliar, but procrastination is no solution to that problem.

Most of us feel anxious when we have to try something new and unfamiliar, but procrastination is no solution to that problem. Indeed, putting things off may only make them seem worse than they really are.

DEALING WITH PROCRASTINATION

It was Howard's senior year in college. He knew it was time to start making plans for his life after graduation. Some of his friends were already lining up jobs at large companies. Howard's parents had already warned him that he would have to support himself once college was over. But Howard was having such a good time on campus that he didn't want to think about next year.

Anyway, the entire process of looking for a job seemed so overwhelming; he just couldn't face it.

─────────── **EXERCISE** ───────────

Are you a procrastinator? If you answer yes to two or more of these statements, you probably are.

■ I regularly put off unpleasant projects and concentrate on doing what I enjoy.

■ I often feel overwhelmed by a new, unfamiliar assignment and put off starting it.

■ I can usually find a reason for not getting down to my work.

■ I'm easily distracted from my work by interruptions.

■ I always seem to run out of time and never finish a project by the deadline.

■ I enjoy living on the edge and leaving assignments until the last minute.

■ Friends and coworkers often tell me I should start projects sooner.

When you're dragging your feet on a task that seems endless or insurmountable, break it down into simpler components.

—Stephanie Winston in *The Organized Executive*

How can Howard start to deal with this situation and conquer the problem of procrastination? The best approach is to take it one step at a time. Otherwise, it's easy to feel overwhelmed. Howard might begin slowly, by having a conversation with his college career counselor. Perhaps they could explore areas that might complement his skills and interests. Then Howard could try an internship in one of these areas. By working part time as an intern, he can find out if he really likes the work. The internship also gives him valuable hands-on experience that can prove very appealing to an employer when Howard looks for a full-time job after graduation.

As a next step, Howard might attend various career fairs and talk to companies that are hiring recent college graduates. This experience might help him target several prospective employers. Finally, he might send out his resume and a cover letter to each of these companies and arrange employment interviews.

By breaking down the process into small steps, Howard can accomplish all of them—one by one. In this way, job hunting won't seem so overwhelming. He can put each step on his schedule for specific times throughout the year. Then he can accomplish the steps without putting off the job-hunting process until the last minute. By that time, it is likely to be too late: The opportunities for internships will have passed, the job fairs will be over, and Howard will find himself far less likely to find a job that appeals to him.

Many people feel overwhelmed by a long writing project, such as a term paper. They look at a blank computer screen and wonder how they will ever write the assigned number of pages. If you approach the task that way, you can easily defeat yourself before

---

STEPS TO STOPPING PROCRASTINATION

1. Realize that you are unnecessarily delaying a project or assignment.

2. Identify and list the true reasons why you are hesitant to start.

3. Overcome these reasons by being focused and determined to change.

4. Start the task.

Source: California Polytechnic State University

you start. A better approach is to tackle the term paper section by section. Each section has to be only a few pages long. Set a deadline for yourself and finish each section by the deadline. You might even break each section up into several parts, spending a few hours every day on each one. Before you know it, you've completed an entire section. Then you begin thinking about the next section, and write it the same way. The term paper seems far less daunting if you break it up into small pieces. You're much less likely to get panicked this way than if you try to think about writing the whole project at once.

Although you may feel overwhelmed by a new task, don't succumb to procrastination like this worker. To stop procrastinating, break large projects up into many parts and reward yourself when you finish them. (Corbis)

Breaking a large project into many pieces is an effective method of beating procrastination. For example, Rachel Anderson, a college senior, used to work part time at a coffee and bagel shop. Her responsibilities included making sandwiches, cleaning up the store at the end of the day, and setting up for the next morning.

Breaking a large project into many pieces is an effective method of beating procrastination.

It was a demanding job that clearly left no room for procrastination. Rachel had to break down some of the tasks into manageable pieces in order to get them all done. She then scheduled these tasks for various times throughout the day.

For example, Rachel was given a half-hour to close up the shop. In order to get everything done on time, she put away the tablecloths after customers had finished eating in the afternoon. Once she finished with the sandwich boards at lunch and no longer needed them, she immediately cleaned the boards and put them away. She also brought up the cleaning supplies early so they would be ready when she had to mop the floor. By completing tasks step by step and not leaving them until the last minute, she had plenty of time to get everything done.

The following sections describe several other tips that will help you beat the pitfalls of procrastination.

DON'T PUT OFF AN UNPLEASANT TASK

Suppose you're late shipping an order, and you have to call an unhappy customer. This is never a pleasant prospect, so no one wants to do it. However, putting it off doesn't make it any easier. Indeed, if you spend

TAKE A BREAK

In order to stay on track and get every-thing done at work, you should take a few small breaks throughout the day, if possible. Here are some suggestions on how to take a few minutes to regain your focus:

■ Go for a walk to get some fresh air and clear your mind.

■ Read a book or magazine.

■ Write a short letter to a friend.

■ Write a list of what you have to do after work, the meals you want to cook this week, or another topic that is unrelated to work.

■ Clear old emails from your inboxes and outboxes.

■ Catch up on current events by reading a newspaper or news website.

After a refreshing break, it should be easier for you to stay focused and concentrate on your work tasks.

the entire day anticipating that call, it will only seem worse. Instead, do it early in the day. This is often the time when you're fresher and you have the most energy. It will probably be easier to get the task accomplished.

REWARD YOURSELF

After you complete an unpleasant task, give yourself a pat on the back. Do something enjoyable. Take a break or have a snack. Make a telephone call to a friend and chat for a few minutes. This is a good way to put the unpleasantness behind you and get on with the rest of your day. Next, work on a more enjoyable task to give your mind a break. You will find that it is easier to get work done when you don't have a difficult task looming over you.

After you complete an unpleasant task, give yourself a pat on the back.

TAKE ACTION

Sometimes a task seems so complex that it's hard to know where to start. In this type of situation, it's easy to become immobilized and do nothing. You keep putting off the project and procrastinating until the deadline is finally staring you in the face. Then you panic and do a poor job.

Sometimes you have to approach a new task through trial and error. Suppose your boss wants you to come up with a new form for ordering supplies. "This isn't my job," you say to yourself. "Why did he ask me?" But your boss isn't the type of person who likes to be questioned when he makes a decision. First, you try not to think about the project. Maybe he'll change his mind and forget it. But as the days go by, he keeps asking you about the new form. Finally, you realize that you have to start somewhere. So you talk to people at your company who deal with suppliers and ask for their advice. Little by little you gather information. Some of it is useful; some isn't. You experiment with several new designs for the form. Eventually, by trial and error, you figure out an approach that may satisfy your boss, and you create the new form.

MAINTAIN YOUR PRIORITIES

If you make something a top priority, chances are you'll get it done. Constantly review your to-do list for the day and the week. Look at your schedule. Determine your top priorities and stay focused on them. This will enable you to get the most important items accomplished.

Determine your top priorities and stay focused on them. This will enable you to get the most important items accomplished.

EXERCISE

If you're a procrastinator, now is the time to change your habits. If you have a lengthy task, break it down into bite-size pieces. Then put each piece on your weekly schedule.

If a task seems complicated, take action and start somewhere. Deal with an unpleasant task early in the day, instead of putting it off. And make sure to stay focused on your priorities.

Keep a log for the next month. Use the tips discussed in this section. Are you completing tasks sooner and more efficiently? Do you complete more of them before the deadlines?

ARE YOU A PERFECTIONIST?

By his own admission, Darryl was a perfectionist. He was always looking for just the right line to start a report. And he wouldn't begin until he found it. As a result, he often procrastinated. He'd put off a report until the last minute and frequently miss a deadline completely.

Darryl also failed to prioritize things effectively. For example, he would often put as much energy into writing an email to one of his coworkers as he did into an important memo to his boss. From his point of view, both the email and memo had to be perfect. Darryl would spend hours and hours at his desk going over his written work until it was absolutely flawless. Long after everyone else had left, he was still working.

Perfection can't be expected in this world.

—Old proverb

The search for perfection often turns responsible people into procrastinators. It also prevents them from prioritizing their work successfully. Some tasks, like Darryl's email, simply don't need to be done perfectly. Others demand a much a higher standard, like Darryl's memo to his boss. If you try to make everything perfect, you'll end up driving yourself crazy. What's more, you're apt to put in needless hours of work that could be spent on something more important.

If you're like Darryl, you can deal with this problem by using the same approach discussed in Chapter 3 in regard to telephone calls. Evaluate your tasks according to the three criteria: essential, time-limited, and unimportant. Essential tasks

HOW TO DEAL WITH PERFECTIONISM

- Realize that people won't think any less of you because you're not perfect—they aren't perfect either.

- Recognize that nothing is ever perfect; it can merely be improved.

- Be kind to yourself. Accept a little less than perfection.

- Don't give a project more than the time it really deserves.

- Reward yourself for a job well done.

If you're a perfectionist, start by putting less pressure on yourself.

require the highest standards of excellence and usually the most time. But even these may never reach perfection. If you're a perfectionist, start by putting less pressure on yourself. Accept a little less. You'll be much happier.

PROCRASTINATORS CAN CHANGE

"I used to be a procrastinator," admits Carol Peterson. "I stopped. I felt overwhelmed and hated that feeling."

You can stop being a procrastinator, too. First, accept the fact that the projects you're putting off aren't going away. By worrying about them, they'll often seem harder. And by leaving them until the last minute, you often won't get them done as successfully.

You'll use your time much more effectively if you work on ways to overcome procrastination. Don't let large projects overcome you. Divide them into manageable parts and take breaks to regain focus. Treat unpleasant projects just as you would a swim in cold water—jump right in. It's often easier to get it over with as quickly as possible. And if perfectionism is causing you to procrastinate, settle for a slightly lower standard.

Treat unpleasant projects just as you would a swim in cold water— jump right in.

As one writer put it: "Procrastination is the art of keeping up with yesterday." This is another way of saying that procrastination always makes you feel as if you're behind. If you want to get ahead, eliminate procrastination.

IN SUMMARY . . .

In this chapter you've learned to avoid procrastination in the following ways:

- Start with a small project that you've been putting off.
- Break assignments up into small steps.

- Keep your priorities in check. Chances are that you'll dive head first into a task that you've made a top priority.

- When you complete a project, take time to enjoy the satisfaction of completion, and reward yourself.

- Don't become obsessed with perfection. Striving for perfection often prevents responsible people from prioritizing their work and causes them to procrastinate.

- Don't put off difficult or unpleasant projects.

- Don't expect to transform your habits overnight. Developing new habits takes time.

5

ORGANIZING YOUR WORKPLACE

"**C**arol, how do you ever find anything in here?" Jim asked, as they sipped their coffee together in her tiny office.

"I can't help it if I'm not a neat freak like you are," she smiled. "I've got other priorities." Throughout the company, Carol's office was generally referred to as "the pit." There was paper lying everywhere. It was falling off the windowsills. Files bulging with paper were stacked on the chairs. Paper skyscrapers rose from the floor. Carol's desk was covered with papers, leaving barely an inch of space on which she could do her work.

"I'll clean it up someday," she kept telling herself. But someday never came. Indeed, the mess in her office grew worse and worse. What Carol didn't seem to realize was that she wasted precious time hunting for important files that were hidden away under stacks of paper. Since she was never quite sure where the files might be—or, for that matter, if they were even in her office at all—it made the task of locating them very stressful. The additional stress made her job much more difficult than it had to be.

One morning Carol was sitting behind an enormous pile of papers on her desk. She was putting the final touches on her segment of an important presentation—a presentation she and her work team had to make to their boss, the vice president of manufacturing. "Are you almost ready?" Jim asked, sticking his head inside Carol's office. "We're due to go on in less than half an hour."

"Yes, I'm all set," she answered. Jim came over to her desk and together they looked over the material she had prepared. Suddenly, he noticed that something was missing.

"Where are those figures you received from the Department of Commerce in Washington?" he asked. "We can't make this presentation without them." Frantically, Carol and Jim went through everything in the folder, but the figures weren't there.

"I know they're here somewhere," Carol said. Jim looked around the office. "How will we ever find them in this mess?" he asked. "Come on!" she pleaded. "They've got to be here. Help me look." Carol began digging through the stacks of paper on her desk, desperately searching for the missing figures.

Meanwhile, Jim frantically skimmed through the files on the windowsill. Then he started looking through the piles of paper on the floor.

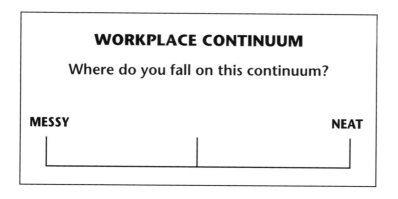

Finally, Jim shook his head. "It's no use," he sighed. "We don't have more time."

Carol was very upset. "How could I do this? The whole team was counting on me and I let them down."

NEATNESS COUNTS

Some people like working in a messy environment. They seem to thrive in chaos. Perhaps they're fortunate enough to have a willing assistant—someone who keeps them on track, ensures that they meet their deadlines, and prevents them from drowning under a pile of paperwork. However, you're not likely to have such a person in school or on your first job. It's completely up to you to keep yourself organized.

FACT

Employees spend as much as one hour each day searching for papers on their desks.

Perhaps you're one of those people who convince themselves that they can always find what they need amid the clutter in their workspace. Sometimes you can, but often it happens only after a lengthy search. More often than not, you aren't so lucky and lose something important, just the way Carol did.

How do you deal with this problem? The first step is to make a note on your to-do list. In big letters, write: CLEAN UP WORK SPACE. Make it a top priority. Put it on your schedule and set aside enough time to get it done. As you clean up the books and papers strewn around your work area, you may even discover at least one or two items you thought were lost forever. Perhaps you'll find a treasured piece of jewelry that slipped under a pile of papers or a prized pen that rolled underneath some books. Getting organized can have a lot of benefits.

This doesn't mean that you have to become a neat freak. You don't need to clean off every space, arrange all your files in a row, or carefully align all the books in your bookcase. While some people may like this type of order, it isn't necessary to manage your projects successfully. What will help, however, is an effective method of organizing your materials so you can find them quickly and work with them as easily as possible.

A SIMPLE FILING SYSTEM

The best way to stay organized at work is to develop a simple filing system. You might begin by organizing the papers in your workspace according to three categories: *essential, lower priority,* and *unimportant.*

Essential papers deal with projects that you're currently working on—those assignments with the highest priority. Each of these should be given its own file folder with the name of the assignment carefully marked on it. For example, "Civil War Report" might be the title of one folder; keep all the papers related to that project inside this folder. Since this is an essential, high-priority project, this folder should probably remain on your desk.

The best way to stay organized at work is to develop a simple filing system.

Maintain an organized file system like this worker has done so you don't waste time searching for documents. (Corbis)

Some people rely on an "inbox" to help them with their filing system. Attorney Karen Jeffers uses a three-tiered box. On the top level are her pending files and papers. These refer to essential, high-priority projects that she is currently working on. Pending matters also appear on Karen's to-do list for the week. On the second level are projects that have lower priority. They don't have to be done immediately. She puts the deadlines for these projects on her calendar to ensure that they will eventually be accomplished.

But the deadlines aren't immediate. These projects might be handled next week or next month. On the lowest level of the inbox are papers marked "to the file." These refer to unimportant matters. Perhaps they are projects that have already been handled.

Instead of leaving these papers out to clutter her office, Jeffers regularly puts them away in her filing cabinets. Every file in these cabinets is carefully marked according to the specific project. Then any papers related to that project can be placed in the appropriate file.

To stay organized, go through your file cabinets periodically to clear out old or unimportant papers. Mark the date on your calendar when you do this, and clean out the folders every few months so they don't get filled with outdated information.

FACT

Less than half of the paper that finds its way to your desk on the job is worth your attention.

There is one final category of paper—*trash*. "If you don't need a paper any longer, put it in the recycling bin or throw it away," explains author Jeffrey Mayer. Much of the paper we receive every day is useless, yet we often seem reluctant to get rid of it. Take mail, for example. A great deal of it consists of catalogs or other kinds of junk mail, trying to persuade us to buy something. How many of these products are you ever likely to purchase? Yet the letters and catalogs often hang around week after week because you never get around to throwing them away.

Perhaps you receive letters from friends. Some should be answered immediately. Others may need no answer at all. But after a certain length of time, most letters don't have to be kept around any longer. They simply fill up your work area and should be discarded. You may also find yourself keeping papers and research materials from old projects completed months ago. Most of these may have little or no

Much of the paper we receive every day is useless, yet we often seem reluctant to get rid of it.

EXERCISE

If your work area is filled with papers and files, now is the time to start bringing some order to this chaos. Organize the material according to the three-category system: essential, lower priority, and unimportant. Then add the fourth category—trash. Use the "1 in 20" rule. If you haven't looked at the item once in the last 20 days, put it in a file cabinet or throw it out.

value; they simply take up space. By throwing them out, you can reduce the clutter in your workspace enormously, in addition to the unnecessary stress that such clutter brings to your workday.

KEEP NOTES TO A MINIMUM

Tom's office looked like an autumnal woodland setting: There was a forest of little colored notes—yellow, green, pink, and orange—pasted everywhere. They were hanging on the walls, bookcases, desk, and file cabinet. They contained telephone numbers, reminders to do something, or important statistics for a report. Unfortunately, there were too many notes in too many places, and Tom usually forgot to look at any of them. Or if he did need to find a specific note, he had to search the entire room before locating it.

Bringing order to your notes is just as important as organizing your files. Some notes can probably be thrown in the wastebasket because you no longer need them. Others may relate to a particular project that has already been completed. They can be put in the appropriate folder for that project inside your file cabinet. Other notes may refer to priority projects that you are currently handling. These should be placed in the appropriate files in your inbox. Of course, there are always a few notes that relate to very

To avoid being overwhelmed with paper files, be selective when deciding which memos and other documents to keep. (Corbis)

significant matters for which you have no file. These might include a telephone number for someone you recently met and plan to call for lunch. This type of note might be put on a small corkboard near your desk so you can refer to it easily. Better yet, you can add important contact information to your address book or phone list to avoid misplacing such a note.

HALLMARKS OF CLUTTER CHAMPIONS

■ The floors in their rooms never see the light of day because they're covered with books and dirty clothes.

■ Their desks look like dumping grounds for old papers.

■ Their trash baskets are overflowing and haven't been emptied in weeks.

■ Their computers are filled with loads of unnecessary files that they no longer use.

■ Their offices are piled high with stacks of unfinished projects.

■ Their to-do lists and weekly schedules are never updated because no one can find them.

■ Their notes are pasted up everywhere and no one looks at them.

Bringing order to your notes is just as important as organizing your files.

When it comes to organizing notes and papers, the one guideline you should always remember is BE SELECTIVE. There isn't room to keep everything out in front of you. Some of it may belong on your desk. Some belongs in a file cabinet. And the rest probably should be thrown away.

The same rule applies to files on your computer. People often fill up their hard drives with useless files that they no longer need. Many of these can be deleted. Others can be transferred to disks and stored in small filing cabinets on a bookshelf. This leaves your hard drive available for the really important items.

AVOID ELECTRONIC CLUTTER

In addition to organizing a traditional paper mess, you should also avoid clutter in your email accounts and voicemailboxes. Don't save messages unless they are truly important and you will need to refer to them. Or to make sure your inbox doesn't fill up, print or write important information from emails and then delete them. It will be useful to have hard copies of these messages—you don't want to lose essential information to a virus or other electronic glitch. Most inboxes have a quota, so if you get careless about deleting unimportant messages and emptying your trash, you might never get important mail, since your box is full and bounces all new messages back. Most email programs also enable you to create folders in which you can store emails related to a specific project, person, or topic. This type of sorting will also help you keep your inbox in order.

Disorganized, random messages on your phone or email accounts take a long time to sift through. In addition, you might easily forget to reply to an important request if there are 200 other messages in your inbox. To save yourself the time and trouble, make sure that your inboxes are cleaned out frequently.

If we had time to organize, we'd be less harried. But if we were less harried, we'd have time to organize.

—**Richard Laliburte, writer**

ORGANIZE WHAT YOU READ

In the workplace, information comes at us from everywhere. Some of it is valuable, but much of it isn't. How do you keep your workspace from becoming a large storage closet, filled with piles of magazines and newspapers? Once again, you have to learn to be selective and keep only the material that you need.

Some people maintain an article file. They clip magazine and newspaper articles that may relate to their projects and place all of them in a single file. They then throw away the papers and magazines. While this cuts down on the clutter in their offices, it may create another problem. After a short period of time, the file is bulging with all types of articles. And finding one related to a specific subject requires looking through the entire file.

One freelance book writer uses a different approach: He creates a file for each book he's writing. Every time he sees an article related to the book's subject, he clips the article and puts it in the appropriate file. He may work on each chapter of the book several weeks or even months apart—in between working on other projects. But when he eventually starts writing, the article he needs is right there in the file.

THE HOME OFFICE

Sandy's company needed to save some money. They decided to close the regional sales office where Sandy

---

EXERCISE

As you are assigned writing projects in school, begin to clip articles from newspapers and magazines that relate to these projects. Start a file for each project. Put the articles in the appropriate files so they'll be there when you need them.

A home office can be a very productive workspace as long as it is well lit, organized, and located away from distractions. (Corbis)

and her colleagues worked. All of the employees were asked to work out of offices at home. Sandy had mixed feelings about working at home. She liked the freedom it provided, but she was concerned whether she'd have the discipline necessary to get all her tasks done each day.

FACT

One survey showed that almost three-fourths of employees feel they are more productive when working at home than in an office.

PROS AND CONS OF THE HOME OFFICE

There are many things to consider when deciding where to work. In order to succeed in a home-office setting, you should set strict hours for your workday. Working from home has several pros and cons.

Pros

- Clients get more personal attention.

- There are fewer interruptions from clients dropping by as they would in an office.

- The atmosphere is more private and more comfortable.

Cons

- There are no face-to-face interactions with coworkers.

- Working at home requires more self-motivation.

- You may find more distractions at home.

Many people feel the way Sandy does, although more and more of them are working from home. Some of these people set the same schedules for themselves that they would keep in an office. They start work at eight or nine o'clock in the morning, take a break for lunch, and continue working until

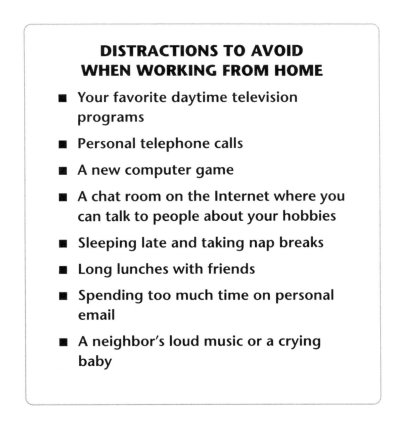

DISTRACTIONS TO AVOID WHEN WORKING FROM HOME

- Your favorite daytime television programs
- Personal telephone calls
- A new computer game
- A chat room on the Internet where you can talk to people about your hobbies
- Sleeping late and taking nap breaks
- Long lunches with friends
- Spending too much time on personal email
- A neighbor's loud music or a crying baby

five or six in the evening. This helps them avoid the temptation of staying in bed late or taking the afternoon off and not completing all of their work. They also try to avoid the distractions or time wasters dis-

---

EXERCISE

Many of the same items you need for a home office are necessary for the space where you do your homework. Do you have all of them?

- Sturdy desk

- Comfortable chair

- Strong light source

- Handy file cabinet and folders

- Desk calendar

- Organizer for paper clips, pens, rubber bands, tape, etc.

- Corkboard

- In/out boxes

- Telephone

- Computer with Internet access

cussed in Chapter 3. They don't allow themselves to waste much time on unimportant telephone calls. If a friend drops over for a chat, they keep these conversations limited.

People with home offices also try to create a workspace for themselves that is entirely user-friendly. Are you a person who likes to look outside while you work? If so, you should put your office in a room with a window. Select a sturdy desk for yourself and a comfortable chair. Make sure the important items are easy to reach, such as the telephone, computer, or fax machine.

You'll also need an inbox and a handy file cabinet. Some people like to keep small organizers on their desks to keep track of important items such as paper clips, pens, rubber bands, and tape. A desk calendar is essential to maintaining your schedule, and a corkboard allows you to post a few notes.

KEEP YOUR WORK AREA ORGANIZED

Organizing your work area will increase your efficiency and enable you to accomplish more in less time. The key to organizing paper is learning how to be selective. This means keeping only the highest priority items on your desk. Unimportant items that you no longer need should be thrown out.

The rest can be put in your filing cabinet. A good filing system is essential because it will help you find notes and articles when you need them. It will also enable you to keep piles of paper from growing all over your work area.

Finally, the workspace itself should be user-friendly, so you'll want to spend time there doing your projects. Remember, where you work does make a difference— a difference that can lead to greater success.

You may wish to put out one or two personal photographs, showing you with your friends or members of your family. You might also decide to display a small award that you won in school. But don't get carried away and display large posters or calendars. They may look tacky or become distracting. Your company may even have a policy against hanging these things in your office.

Store all of your contact information (including telephone numbers, addresses, and email addresses) in a Rolodex organizer, database, or address book. Or post an organized list of telephone numbers in your office. Don't store important business numbers on your cell phone only—write them down or make a note of them somewhere in case something happens to your phone.

Keep a calendar at work and another one at home. It is easiest to stay organized if you also carry a datebook or daily planner. Having your schedule with you at all times is useful in case you need to check dates and add new ones. Mark events even if they aren't set in stone; keeping a record of pending events is a sure way to avoid overscheduling.

IN SUMMARY . . .

■ Maintaining a clean workspace is extremely important. You will waste a lot of time if you have to search for documents on a cluttered desk.

■ Develop a simple filing system by dividing papers into three categories: essential, lower priority, and unimportant.

■ Be selective when organizing your notes. Once you get out of the habit of saving everything, it will be easier to restore order to your life.

■ If you are working from home, make sure you have a stable desk, comfortable chair, and a file cabinet. An inbox and corkboard will also help you organize your workspace.

■ Avoid distractions when working at home, such as daytime television and long phone conversations.

■ Keep only the highest priority items on your desk.

■ A cluttered workspace looks unprofessional and adds stress to your daily work.

SEVEN SECRETS OF BETTER TIME MANAGEMENT

It was almost midnight and Sharon was still studying. "If I can only get through these last few pages of notes, I know I'll get an A on that test," she thought as her eyes started to close.

Sharon was an intensely focused student. She kept to a very rigorous schedule, with little time for anything else but work. For example, she regularly spent three to four hours on her homework per night. Sharon set high standards for herself, accepting nothing less than the best. Or perhaps it would be more accurate to say that her parents would accept nothing less from her. They expected her to get into a top-rated college. And after graduation, Sharon's father expected that she would follow in his footsteps and become a doctor.

To be accepted at a prestigious college, Sharon not only had to excel in academics; she had to participate in various extracurricular activities. As sports editor of the school newspaper, she covered varsity games and wrote detailed articles on them. She was also captain of the school debate team. Both activities were extremely time consuming. When she wasn't studying, Sharon was preparing for a debate or putting the finishing touches on an article about a recent basketball game.

Sharon seemed to be working constantly. "It's the price you have to pay for success," her parents told her. "And we want you to be successful." Was this the way Sharon wanted to go through high school—working herself sometimes to the point of exhaustion? She never really asked herself that question. She didn't have time.

STEP 1: LEAVE TIME FOR PERSONAL GOALS THAT ARE IMPORTANT TO YOU

Many people seem to put heavy demands on themselves. Surveys tell us that U.S. employees are more productive today than at any time in the past. We no sooner complete one task than we start another. Indeed, many people have become skilled at "multitasking," that is, doing several things at one time, such as reading the newspaper, eating breakfast, and watching television.

In the 19th century, the French writer Alexis de Tocqueville observed that Americans always seemed to be in a hurry. Little has changed since that time. We seem intent on cramming as much as possible into every day. But very few of us stop to ask whether these are the things we really want to be doing or whether our actions really satisfy our personal goals.

U.S. employees are more productive today than at any time in the past.

The day you put your goal in writing is the day it becomes a commitment that will change your life.

—Tom Hopkins, sales trainer and founder of Tom Hopkins International

A good schedule can help us organize the tasks we do each day, but it cannot tell us what those tasks ought to be. We have to make those decisions ourselves. If you're planning to attend college and embark on a satisfying career, you'll need to study hard, just the way Sharon did. But make sure you also leave time for yourself. Build in time for quiet reflection, evaluate what you're doing, and ask yourself whether you're on the right track. Perhaps Sharon was happy with her busy schedule. On the other hand, she may have wanted to spend more time doing something else.

Don't let your schedule get so rigid that you can't allow yourself an opportunity to change. Suppose

━━━━━━━━━━ **EXERCISE** ━━━━━━━━━━

What is the most important personal goal you would like to achieve? What steps have you taken to attain it? What else could you be doing to reach this objective?

Sharon wanted to learn to play a musical instrument or just spend more time hanging out with her friends. This may have taken time away from another activity—time she may have been afraid to give up for fear of disappointing her parents. It's easy to let time slip away and find yourself carrying out someone else's priorities. As you organize your days and weeks, set aside enough hours to do what you think is important.

Time wasted is existence; used, is life.

—Edward Young, 18th-century English poet

STEP 2: DON'T OVERSCHEDULE YOURSELF

"I overschedule myself and then feel bad if I don't get everything done," explains career counselor Carol

Peterson. Indeed, many people try to take on so much that there aren't enough hours in a day to handle all of it.

According to a study by Professor Roger Buehler and his colleagues, people regularly underestimate how long it will take to complete a project and therefore don't leave enough time for it. The study showed that the participants' time estimates may have been off by as much as three weeks for long-term projects such as a senior thesis. And they may have underestimated the time for a shorter project, such as repairing an automobile, by as much as three days.

Buehler points out that the same problems exist on the job. Employees tend to be overly optimistic about the time it will take to get something done. They over-schedule themselves, promise too much, and don't leave enough time to get their projects accomplished.

One way to deal with this problem is to recall similar tasks that you had to do in the past. For example, what kinds of obstacles did you face in writing a report for your supervisor? Did it take you longer to collect all the necessary research data than you thought it would? Did you need to obtain information from coworkers who were out of town and unavailable? Thinking about all the hurdles that had to be overcome in the past may be enough to persuade you to build in some extra time when undertaking a similar project.

Two executives put the finishing touches on a project. In order to complete quality work, don't overschedule, and don't try to finish important tasks at the last minute. (Corbis)

As you estimate the amount of time required to do a project, don't forget to build in another 10 percent for Murphy's Law, which states: Anything that can go wrong will go wrong. A computer glitch, for example, can wreak havoc with any schedule. A traffic jam can make you late for an appointment unless you've allowed yourself some extra time to get there.

In addition, remember to factor in family obligations and health concerns when you make your schedule. You never know when things may come up, so it is a good idea to leave yourself a little room in case something does. If you pack your schedule too tightly, trying to get back on track after an emergency hits could be disastrous.

EXERCISE

- Do you try to schedule too many things in too little time? If so, how does it make you feel? What could you do to schedule yourself more successfully?

- Recall a time when you were working on a project and something happened that threw off your entire schedule. How did you cope with it?

- Make a list of five things that could go wrong as you work on a project. Then make a list of what you would do in those situations. Brainstorming will prepare you to act quickly and get back on track if something does go wrong.

Expect the unexpected; then be prepared to deal with it. Nick had carefully prepared a slide show to present to new employees as part of their orientation program. As he flipped on the projector, the light bulb blew out. Unfortunately, a spare bulb wasn't readily available and the entire presentation had to be postponed. Nick was embarrassed and he made a negative impression on the new employees. Once again, Murphy's Law had claimed a victim.

People who are well organized have learned how to prepare for the unexpected. This means not only building in extra time to deal with unanticipated

KNOWING THE SCORE

Don Wetmore gives seminars on time management. One time-management tip he practices is making a long list of his activities and grading them from A to D. He makes a new list every six months and cuts down on activities that score less than Bs. According to Wetmore, most people spend about 80 percent of their time on Cs and Ds.

Source: *Chicago Tribune*

problems, but using some of that time to prevent problems from turning into disasters. Bulbs often have a way of blowing out when you turn on a slide projector to present your first slide. Jim should have taken a few moments to round up an extra light bulb in advance of the presentation. This just takes a little planning.

STEP 3: DO IT RIGHT THE FIRST TIME

It's far less time consuming to do something right the first time than to go back and do it over and over again.

U.S. companies recognize the importance of producing quality products. This means making them right the first time—without any defects that need to be repaired. If they want to keep a customer coming back, companies realize that they must build products such as computers, automobiles, and dishwashers that run effectively. Companies also know that it costs less to make a product right the first time rather than to repair it.

The same principle applies when you do your work. It's far less time consuming to do something right the first time than to go back and do it over and over again. It also earns you far higher marks with your supervisor.

Many of us seem to put too much emphasis on speed. Somehow, faster always seems to be better. However, if you try to complete a task too quickly, you're apt to make mistakes—mistakes that will cost you time and energy later. You may feel like an effective worker when you finish projects quickly, but your employer won't if you often have to redo things. Slow down and build a little extra time into your schedule to review your work and revise it if necessary. This will enable you to submit a much better product.

─────── EXERCISE ───────

Think of a project that you tried to complete too fast. Ask yourself the following questions:

- **What was the result?**

- **How did you feel about it?**

- **How did others feel about the quality of your work?**

- **How could you have approached the project in a more efficient manner?**

- **If you're working on a project now, what can you do to avoid needless mistakes in it? List the steps you'll need to take to complete this project.**

STEP 4: PUT YOUR SCHEDULE IN WRITING AND MAKE IT SPECIFIC

In order to organize your time effectively, don't trust your memory. You must write everything down.

In order to organize your time effectively, don't trust your memory. You must write everything down. As soon as you receive an assignment, put it on your to-do list. Look at the other things you have to accomplish and determine whether this new assignment should be given a higher priority. Perhaps something else on your to-do list can wait and just as easily be done later. Bump this project to another day and replace it with the new one that has a more important priority. Then give this higher priority project the time slot on your schedule that was previously filled by the lower priority item.

If your schedule is shifting regularly and you need to handle a variety of projects, you must be as specific about them as possible. Suppose you're working on several assignments for your supervisor. With the hectic schedule that you must maintain at your office, you realize that it will be necessary to work on at least one of these projects at home. So you make a note on your schedule for Thursday night: "Work on project." Thursday arrives and you look at your schedule. You put the project notes in your briefcase and head for home. Unfortunately, you picked up the notes for the wrong project. This one has a much lower priority than the one you're sup-

EXERCISE

Look at your schedule for the week. How specific have you been in writing down each assignment? If an assignment is to be done three or four days from now, will you clearly understand what you're supposed to do by the time you get to it?

pose to be doing. So you must go back to the office and pick up the notes, wasting precious time.

That's why it is so important to make your schedule specific. When you made up the schedule at the beginning of the week, it may have seemed obvious which project you were going to do on Thursday. But by the time Thursday arrives, you have forgotten your schedule. Why depend on your memory when it's so easy to write everything down? A few extra seconds spent making your schedule specific can save you far more time later.

FACT

The National Association of Professional Organizers was founded in 1987 and now has more than 1500 members. The association is divided into subspecialties, including Time Management, Goal Setting, Filing Systems, and many others. To learn more, visit http://www.naponet.net.

STEP 5: HAVE A PLACE FOR EVERYTHING

Disorganized people constantly seem to be looking for things they can't find. Perhaps it's an important paper that's disappeared from their files. Or it may be a vital telephone number that suddenly seems to be missing just when they need it most. If you're one of these people, you should select some convenient places to put materials and routinely store them there. Then you're likely to find the information when it's needed.

As explained earlier, high-priority files might be placed in your inbox and less important ones in your file cabinet. If you've finished working on a file, don't leave it out in your workspace. It might get lost. Return it to your inbox or your file cabinet. Return papers to the appropriate file after you've finished with them. Otherwise they may be lost or misplaced.

When it comes to telephone numbers, some people like to keep them on little slips of paper strewn around their work area, but this is a sure-fire way of losing them. A much more organized approach is to keep a book of telephone numbers and put important new ones in there soon after you receive them. Another handy place to store telephone numbers is on your computer. Many systems have a built-in program for recording names, numbers, and addresses.

It's also a good idea to keep supplies in a convenient location near your desk so they're easily accessible. Instead of hunting around the room for paper clips, scissors, or pens, always keep them in the same place. Use a desk organizer and always put the items back after you use them. This way you don't have to search for them later when you need them again.

—— EXERCISE ——

Look at your workspace and go through a mental checklist. Are your files carefully organized? Are important telephone numbers easy to reach? Are your supplies handy? Is your desk neat enough to get your work done?

STEP 6: PRACTICE SELF-DISCIPLINE

Organized people use a disciplined approach to getting things done. In fact, if you don't improve your self-discipline, you'll never improve your organization

THE KEY ELEMENTS OF SELF-DISCIPLINE

Self-disciplined	Not self-disciplined
Works on projects in the order of their priority	Deals with projects haphazardly and in no particular priority
Routinely completes assignments	Leaves assignments unfinished
Writes down assignments when receiving them	Doesn't write down assignments but tries to remember them
Tries to do projects right the first time	Must usually redo projects to correct mistakes
Creates a schedule and tries to stick to it	Follows no schedule for getting work done
Knows how to say "no" to interruptions	Allows self to be continuously distracted from work
Starts projects as soon as possible and finishes them on time	Procrastinates and regularly misses deadlines
Commits to a manageable number of projects	Overcommits and usually tries to do too much in too little time
Uses small blocks of time creatively to accomplish work	Wastes small blocks of time and accomplishes nothing
Maintains an organized workplace	Works in a disorganized environment

skills. The chart on the opposite page presents the key elements of self-discipline by comparing a self-disciplined person to one who is not. If you possess eight or more of the habits on the self-discipline chart, you are probably self-disciplined at work. If you possess less than eight of these habits, you should evaluate your present habits and see how you might practice more self-discipline.

With self-discipline, all things are possible. Without it, even the simplest goal can seem like an impossible dream.

—Theodore Roosevelt, 26th President of the United States

STEP 7: MONITOR YOUR PROGRESS

Once you've tried out your new schedule, be sure to evaluate it every few weeks. Are you comfortable with everything you have planned or do you often feel overwhelmed? Do you find that you are still wasting time on unimportant tasks? In order to answer these questions and become truly comfortable with your schedule, you should monitor your progress. You may have miscalculated and overscheduled yourself, but it's not the end of the world. As long as you take the time to realize this, you can easily correct it.

SURF THE WEB:
TIME MANAGEMENT

Balance Time
http://www.balancetime.com

Become An Organizer
http://www.becomeanorganizer.com

MyGoals.com
http://www.mygoals.com

Mindtools.com
http://www.mindtools.com/page6.html

National Association of Professional Organizers
http://www.napo.net

Organize Tips
http://www.organizetips.com

Organize Your World
http://www.organizeyourworld.com

Scheduleonline.com
http://www.scheduleonline.com

School of Self-Discipline
http://self-discipline.8m.com

In order to appreciate and enjoy being organized, take the time to question how well your schedule is working for you. You may need to adjust your schedule to make it more flexible.

"Slack off a little," advises Lesley Alderman in *Money* magazine. "Squeeze some time into your schedule to simply chill out," Alderman adds. Reward yourself for a job well done before plunging into the next task. If you're driving yourself too hard, ease up a little bit. If you're distracted too easily, you may need to practice a little self-discipline.

DEVELOP YOUR ORGANIZATION SKILLS

Developing your organization skills is like fine-tuning an engine: It takes some tinkering and adjustment. The seven secrets discussed in this chapter can help. Remember that it's important to be as realistic as possible. Don't overschedule yourself, and be sure to leave some time to pursue your personal goals or to just take it easy. You'll have more time if you put your schedule in writing so you don't have to keep trying to remember it. You'll also pick up valuable extra time if you store everything in its proper place so you don't have to search for it. Do assignments right the first time so they don't have to be done over.

None of these habits is easy—at least, not at first. They require self-discipline. But if you're prepared to monitor yourself regularly and keep making improvements, you will be successful.

IN SUMMARY . . .

- Be sure to leave time for important personal goals.

- Don't schedule an unmanageable number of activities into your week. As you estimate how long projects will take, build in an extra 10 percent of time to account for Murphy's Law.

- Produce quality work the first time so you don't have to waste time redoing it.

- Put your schedule in writing. You are more likely to follow a schedule that is written specifically than you are to follow one that is just in your head.

- Put everything in its place. It is much easier to stay organized if you designate a place for everything.

- Practice self-discipline.

- Monitor your progress so you can see where you're improving and feel a sense of accomplishment. This will also allow you to see which areas still need work.

- In order to enjoy your newly organized life, build relaxation time into your schedule.

GLOSSARY

clutter: unnecessary papers and other objects that are scattered haphazardly throughout an office or home; unorganized people are often surrounded by clutter

downsizing: reducing the size of a company, which usually involves scaling back on the number of people employed at that company; companies often downsize to save money

downtime: time that is used to relax, take a break, or do something enjoyable

essential calls: telephone calls that you must attend to immediately, such as an urgent request from your boss or an emergency involving a family member

filing system: an organized group of file folders that contain past and present projects, reports, and other important papers

high priority: a task or event that is very important; high-priority tasks must be taken care of first; a project that is due tomorrow has a higher priority than a project that is due in three weeks

inbox: a container on your desk for papers, memos, and files

low priority: matters that do not have to be taken care of immediately, such as a project that is not due for several months

Murphy's Law: coined by Edward Murphy, an American engineer, the observation that anything that can go wrong will go wrong

organized: arranged and orderly rather than chaotic and unplanned

overschedule: to plan too many activities into a time frame that is too short; this happens when you overestimate how much time you have

pending files: projects that have not yet been completed; pending files may be high priority or low priority

perfectionism: a need to do every task perfectly, no matter how unimportant it may be

personal goals: ambitions that one hopes to accomplish to gain self-fulfillment

prioritize: to arrange in order of importance

procrastination: the act of putting off tasks and waiting until the last minute to start projects

schedule: organizing the items on your to-do list so they are accomplished in specific time periods

self-discipline: the practice of regulating your actions to improve them

time-limit calls: telephone calls that may be important but that should be handled as quickly as possible

time management: a method of organizing each day so you accomplish your most important tasks

time wasters: distractions that prevent you from doing your work

to-do list: a list of projects, errands, and activities that you want to accomplish in a specified period of time; to-do lists can be daily or weekly, long or short

unimportant calls: telephone calls that are not urgent; a call from a friend who wants to chat about her new hairdo is an example of an unimportant call

user-friendly: easy to deal with; a user-friendly
workspace is comfortable and convenient

BIBLIOGRAPHY

Allen, David. *Getting Things Done: The Art of Stress-Free Productivity.* New York: Penguin, 2003.

Barnes, Emilie. *Simply Organized: The Life You Always Searched for…but Were Too Cluttered to Find.* Eugene, Oreg.: Harvest House Publishers, Inc. 1997.

Bossidy, Larry, Ram Shurman, and Charles Burck. *Execution: The Discipline of Getting Things Done.* Victoria, B.C. (Canada): Crown Publications, Inc., 2002.

Covey, Stephen. *The 7 Habits of Highly Effective People.* New York: Simon & Schuster, 1989.

Douglass, Merrill, and Donna Douglass. *Manage Your Time, Manage Your Work, Manage Yourself.* New York: Amacom, 1993.

Eisenberg, Ronni, and Kate Kelly. *Organize Your Office!: Simple Routines for Managing Your Workspace.* New York: Hyperion Books, 1999.

Emmett, Rita. *The Procrastinator's Handbook: Mastering the Art of Doing It Now.* New York: Walker & Company, 2000.

Griessman, B. Eugene. *Time Tactics of Very Successful People.* New York: McGraw-Hill, 1994.

Kanarek, Lisa. *Everything's Organized.* Franklin Lakes, N.J.: Career Press, Inc. 1996.

Knaus, William. *Do It Now!: Break the Procrastination Habit.* Hoboken, N.J.: John Wiley & Sons, 1998.

Kolberg, Judith. *Conquering Chronic Disorganization.* Squall Press, 1999.

Lagatree, Kirsten M. *Checklists For Life: 104 Lists to Help You Get Organized, Save Time, and Unclutter Your Life.* New York: Random House, 2000.

Lipnack, Jessica. *The Age of the Network: Organizing Principles for the 21st Century.* Hoboken, N.J.: John Wiley & Sons, Inc., 1995.

Livesay, Corrine R. *Getting & Staying Organized.* Des Moines, Iowa: American Media, Inc., 1996.

Mackenzie, Alec. *The Time Trap.* New York: Amacom, 1997.

Morgenstern, Julie. *Time Management From the Inside Out: The Foolproof System for Taking Control of Your Schedule and Your Life.* New York: Henry Holt, 2000.

National Association of Professional Organizers, San Francisco Bay Area Chapter Staff. *Organizing Options: Solutions from Professional Organizers.* San Francisco, Calif.: National Association of Professional Organizers, 1995.

Nelson, Mexico Mike. *Clutter-Proof Your Business: Turn Your Mess Into Success.* Franklin Lakes, N.J.: Career Press, 2002.

Schechter, Harriet. *Let Go Of Clutter.* New York: McGraw-Hill/Contemporary Books, 2000.

Tracy, Brian. *Eat That Frog! 21 Great Ways to Stop Procrastinating and Get More Done In Less Time.* San Francisco, Calif.: Berrett-Koehler Publishers, Inc., 2001.

Vetter, Greg. *Find It In 5 Seconds: Gaining Control in the Information Age.* Seattle, Wash.: Hara Publishing, 1999.

Winston, Stephanie. *The Organized Executive.* Washington, D.C: Georgetown Pub. House, 1996.

Index

A

activities, selecting carefully 18–19
adolescents, overscheduling of 11–12
Alderman, Lesley 125
almanacs 21
Anderson, Rachel 15–16, 18
anger, procrastination and 72
article file 99–100

B

Beaudin, Brian 13
breaks, taking 42, 79
Brown, Helen Gurley 48
Buehler, Roger 112
Burke, Edmund 4
Burns, Peter 19
busyness 27–28, 110

C

Carleton University Procrastination
    Research Group 69
cell phone 53–54, 106
clutter 16, 87–88, 98–99, 128
computers 11, 43–44, 98
Covey, Stephen 19, 34–35

D

deadlines
    breaking projects into smaller tasks
        38
    filing projects by 92–93
    procrastination and 70
    schedule management 25–27
desk 16, 87–88, 105
downsizing 128
downtime 62–63, 125, 128

E

efficient organizations, hallmarks of 1
electronic clutter 98–99
email 51, 53, 58–59
errands, planning 60–61

essential calls 128
etiquette, telephone 51

F

family obligations 113–114
Farrington, Jan 12
filing system
    articles 99–100
    described 91–95, 105–106, 128
    home office 105
    time management 120–121
    untidiness 87–88
Franklin, Benjamin 15

G

Garrison, Phyllis 15, 41
goals 34–36, 111
Gonzalez, Anna 62, 63
Griessman, B. Eugene 31, 62

H

handheld computer devices 43
health, procrastination and 69
home office organization 100–105
Hopkins, Tom 110

I

inbox 92, 95, 105, 120, 129
information, handling more 10–11
instant messaging (IM) 53
Internet use 58–59, 124
interruptions. *See* time wasters

J

Jeffers, Karen 92
Jett, Charles 16, 18
job. *See* workplace organization

L

Laliburte, Richard 64, 99
long-term goals 34–36, 111

M
mail, non-electronic 93–94
Martinez, Angela 33
Mayer, Jeffrey 16, 93
meetings, scheduling 31
Murphy's Law 113, 115, 129

N
National Association of Professional
    Organizers 119–120
National Sleep Foundation 11
neatness 89–91
newspaper deadlines 25–27
notes 31, 95–98

O
O'Malley, Michael 21
optimal work time and 63–64
overscheduling 111–116, 129

P
pending files 129
perfectionism 72, 82–84, 129
personal goals 109–111, 129
Peterson, Carol 29, 31, 56–57, 84–85,
    111–112
phone calls. *See* telephone calls
prioritize
    conversations 56
    defined 129
    filing system 91
    goals, accomplishing 111
    procrastination 81
    setting 36–40, 118–119
    telephone calls 52–53
    time management 13–16, 19
procrastination
    breaks, taking 79
    health and 69
    overcoming 73–78, 84–85
    perfectionism and 82–84
    perils of 8, 67–69, 129

prioritizing 81
reasons for 70–73
tasks, approaching 78, 80–81
Procrastination Research Group Carleton
    University 69
productivity 11, 109–110
progress, monitoring 123–125
projects
    filing 91–93, 95, 100
    goals, leaving time for 34–35
    jumping among 59
    scheduling 2, 118–119
    steps, breaking into smaller 76–77
punctuality 15–16

Q
quality 28–29, 116–117

R
reading material 99–100
rest, time for 125
Riley, Teyonda 56, 57
Roosevelt, Theodore 123

S
schedule
    busyness 27–28
    deadlines, handling 25–27
    defined 129
    long-term goals 34–36
    most effective times 63–64
    overscheduling, avoiding 111–116
    priorities, setting 36–40
    projects 2
    quality, ensuring 28–29
    taking stock 44–45
    tasks, breaking down 33–34, 75–76
    to-do lists 29–32, 34, 39
    weekly 41–44
    writing and specifying 118–120
self-assessment questions 5
self-deprecation, procrastination and 72

self-discipline 121–123, 129
sleep 11–12, 69
small blocks of time, using 62–63
socializing 47–48, 55–58
software, scheduling 43–44
stress, reducing 18

T
talking, time wasted 47–48, 55–58
tasks
  breaking down 33–34, 75–76
  estimating time for 112–114
  jumping among 59
  new, tackling 80–81
technology 11, 43, 98
telephone calls
  cell phone 53–54
  essential 49–50
  etiquette 51
  prioritizing 52–53
  time-limit 50, 52
  wasting time 17, 47
Telephone Doctor, The 51
telephone numbers, storing 106,
  120–121
Theophrastis 19
time-limit calls 50, 52, 129
time management
  defined 129
  filing system 120–121
  four key steps 28
  goals, setting aside time for personal
    109–111
  organization skills, developing 12–13,
    125–126
  prioritizing 13–15
  procrastination and lack of 8–9
  progress, monitoring 123–125
  projects, setting 59
  punctuality 15–16
  quality, ensuring 28–29, 116–117
  scheduling 111–116, 118–120

selecting activities carefully 18–19
self-assessment questions 5
self-discipline and 121–123
sleep habits 11–12
stress, reducing 18
wasting time 2, 16–17, 19
workload, increasing 9–11, 20–23
time wasters
  described 47–49, 129
  Internet overuse 58–59
  optimal work time and 63–64
  planning errands 60–61
  self-discipline and 125
  talking 16–17, 19, 55–58
  telephone calls, managing 49–55
Tocqueville, Alexis de 110
to-do list
  prioritizing 37–38
  sample 45
  scheduling items 29–32, 39, 129
  tasks, breaking down 34
transportation
  errands, organizing 60–61
  small tasks 63
  time, leaving enough 42, 68–69
trash 93–94

U
unimportant calls 129
unpleasant tasks 38, 70–71, 78, 80
user-friendly 129

V
visitors, unexpected 17
volunteer organizations 25–27

W
wasting time. *See* time wasters
websites, time management 124
weekly schedule, developing 41–44
Winston, Stephanie 13, 75

workload, increasing 3, 9–11, 20–23
workplace organization
  benefits of 87–89
  desk 105
  electronic clutter, avoiding 98–99
  filing system 91–95, 105–106
  home office 100–105

neatness 89–91
notes, minimizing 95–98
reading material 99–100

Y
Young, Edward 111